CHANGING SEXUAL VALUES AND THE FAMILY

MONOGRAPH OF FAMILY INSTITUTE OF PHILADELPHIA

Changing Sexual Values and The Family

Edited by

G. PIROOZ SHOLEVAR, M.D.

Associate Professor and Director of Child Inpatient Services
Department of Mental Health Sciences
Hahnemann Medical College and Hospital
Philadelphia, Pennsylvania
and
Co-Director
Clinical School of Family Therapy
Family Institute of Philadelphia
Philadelphia, Pennsylvania

CHARLES C THOMAS · PUBLISHER
Springfield · Illinois · U.S.A.

Published and Distributed Throughout the World by
CHARLES C THOMAS • PUBLISHER
Bannerstone House
301-327 East Lawrence Avenue, Springfield, Illinois, U.S.A.

© *1977, by* CHARLES C THOMAS • PUBLISHER
ISBN 0-398-03519-9
Library of Congress Catalog Card Number: 75-35569

Printed in the United States of America
W-2

Library of Congress Cataloging in Publication Data
Main entry under title:

Changing sexual values and the family.

　　1.　Family psychotherapy.　2.　Sex (Psychology)
I.　Sholevar, G. Pirooz.　II.　Title.
RC488.5.C46　　　　616.8'915　　　　　75-35569
ISBN 0-398-03519-9

This book is dedicated to the memory of our friends Rae Weiner and Jerry Ford.

G.P.S.

CONTRIBUTORS

Jean Barr, M.S.W.
Associate Professor
Department of Mental Health Sciences
Hahnemann Medical College and Hospital
Philadelphia, Pennsylvania

Ivan Boszormenyi-Nagy, M.D.
Professor and Coordinator of Family Therapy
Department of Mental Health Sciences
Hahnemann Medical College and Hospital
Philadelphia, Pennsylvania

Sylvia Claven, Ph.D.
Chairperson, Department of Sociology
St. Joseph's College
Philadelphia, Pennsylvania

Richard Crocco, M.D.
Assistant Professor of Psychiatry
Jefferson University
Philadelphia, Pennsylvania

Ilda Ficher, M.A.
Assistant Professor
Department of Mental Health Sciences
Hanhemann Medical College and Hospital
Philadelphia, Pennsylvania

James L. Framo, Ph.D.
Professor of Psychology
Temple University
Philadelphia, Pennsylvania

Alfred S. Friedman, Ph.D.
Director of Research
Philadelphia Psychiatric Center
Philadelphia, Pennsylvania

C. Jack Friedman, Ph.D.

President, Philadelphia Family Institute
Research Scientist
Philadelphia Psychiatric Center
Philadelphia, Pennsylvania

Samuel Granick, Ph.D.

Research Psychologist
Philadelphia Psychiatric Center
Past President of Pennsylvania Psychology Association
Philadelphia, Pennsylvania

Maury Levy

Managing Editor
Philadelphia Magazine

Anita Lichtenstein, M.S.S.

Coordinator of Family Therapy
Albert Einstein Community Mental Health Center
Philadelphia, Pennsylvania

Margaret Mead, Ph.D.

Author
Curator, Museum of Natural Sciences
New York, New York

Otto Pollak, Ph.D.

Professor of Sociology
University of Pennsylvania
Philadelphia, Pennsylvania

Mel Roman, Ph.D.

Associate Professor of Psychiatry
Albert Einstein College of Medicine
New York

David Rubenstein, M.D.

Professor of Psychiatry
Temple University
Philadelphia, Pennsylvania

Virginia Satir, M.S.W.

Faculty of Johns Hopkins University
Baltimore, Maryland

G. Pirooz Sholevar, M.D.
Associate Professor and Director of Child Inpatient Services
Department of Mental Health Sciences
Hahnemann Medical College and Hospital
Philadelphia, Pennsylvania

Maarten Sibinga, M.D.
Professor of Pediatrics
Temple University
Philadelphia, Pennsylvania

John C. Sonne, M.D.
Clinical Associate Professor
Department of Mental Health Sciences
Hahnemann Medical College and Hospital
Philadelphia, Pennsylvania

Geraldine Spark, M.S.W.
Co-director of Division of Family Psychiatry
Eastern Pennsylvania Psychiatric Institute
Past President of Philadelphia Family Institute
Philadelphia, Pennsylvania

Ross V. Speck, M.D.
Social Psychiatrist, Family Therapist
and Psychoanalyst in Private Practice

Carl Whitaker, M.D.
Professor of Psychiatry
University of Wisconsin
Madison, Wisconsin

ACKNOWLEDGMENTS

I wish to thank Dr. Jack Friedman for his encouragement, Ms. Sheila Cronin for the sketches of the family sculpturing scenes, and Ms. Elizabeth Haitsch and Mrs. Christine Scafonas for their tireless work on the manuscript.

CONTENTS

CHANGING SEXUAL VALUES AND THE FAMILY

1

Introduction

C. Jack Friedman

Some years ago the author presented a paper on the effects of dietary treatment in children with phenylketonuria (PKU), an inherited disease treated by highly restricted diet. The diet is so restricted that these children are allowed practically nothing except sugar, candy, and certain liquids, such as milk. The diet is aimed at preventing brain damage and severe mental retardation; the parents of these children are thus quite uptight over maintaining control. We studied the problem by putting the children and their parents into a room set up like a kitchen with toy appliances, food, and food objects. They were told our purpose was to loosen the child up and allow him to adapt to the situatiton. The first mother whose son eyed a toy chicken in the stove invoked the wrath of God. (We must understand that these mothers were quite tense; they had the problem of handling children with a diet, plus the thought that if the child ate indiscriminately, he would suffer severe mental retardation, brain damage, or both, and be impaired for life.) The first mother told her son that God would punish him if he did not obey her. Eventually he went over to the stove and pulled on the door, and the stove tipped over on him; the mother said that God in fact did punish him for it! Another mother handled her child's natural curiosity when he held up a plastic orange and asked, "What's this?" by saying that it was a ball: "Let's play catch with it." Her approach was to change or transform the object entirely.

Most of the parents ignored the food and acted as though it was not there at all, attempting to avoid it by not naming or labeling anything. At times we saw parents try to stop their children from handling food objects; when this did not work, they began to tell the child to do what the child was already doing. This was very much like the tail-wagging-the-dog phenomenon. In addition to the food objects in the room, there was a hand puppet, a very toothy alligator. Inevitably, we saw the fathers pick up the hand puppet and stand between the child and the food making motions. The children would, strangely enough, burst into tears, obviously threatened. They recognized somehow that beyond the smile and façade of the father's face and his enticement to play, there was an angry and perhaps very frightened man.

Most of the parents in the room with those children, when it comes to sex, could have been our parents. One mother exerted control by invoking morality and God. Another made a secret of the fact that an orange was an orange, just as some parents avoid any kind of reference to sexual behavior or sexual anatomy. Most parents use very strong non-verbal cues to prevent sexual curiosity. In others, there is probably no better counterpart to the "alligator maneuver" than the cultural curio of when a father takes his son or a mother takes her daughter aside to teach about sex, intending to make the child feel very comfortable and inform him or her. The actual effect is to make the child either very scared or perplexed. If there is a central point to these comments, it is that reality and reality contact are precious commodities, and where human sexuality is concerned, we have been anything but genuinely real.

If the young people of today choose to establish their own sexual mores, it is largely to escape a good deal of irrationality that has been imposed upon them; sexual education in our society sometimes strains sanity to the limit. For example, the mother who says she always answers the child honestly—but the subject of sex has never come up; fascinating if you think about it! How long does it take before a parent says to a child, "This is your mouth, this is your ear, your nose."? Parents typically do not wait until a child asks, "What is this?" Moreover, when we consider readiness, the oldest of standardized test of intelligence, the Stanford-Binet, expects an eighteen-month-old to be able to identify parts of the body. By the age of two years, he should be able to say something about what their functions are. Let me cite an extreme example: the author once lived at the edge of a cow pasture in which there were two very happy bulls. There was a woman neighbor down the road who thought that the word *bull* was obscene, so she called bulls "gentleman cows"— now that strikes me as a conceptual perversion. What a parent may do in misleading a child about sex is of considerably less consequence than the damage that indirection, suppression, and confusion eventually do to their relationship. We all acquire sexual information at some point or other, but the real damage, I think, is to the parent-child relationship. Like the parent in the simulated kitchen with the PKU child, tense about the breakdown of control and resultant brain damage and mental retardation, the parent faced with following our cultural model of sex education of the child is under maximum risk of using growth and psychological growth-stunting types of maneuvers. When a mother and daughter implicitly recognize their mutual secrecy, the relationship between them cannot help but be a problem. Let me cite another case example.

Some time ago I saw an eleven-year-old girl whose presenting problem was thought to be a school phobia. She had gone through a phase of stomach pains and nausea and vomiting which was followed by an extremely irrational refusal and fearfulness of school. At this point, her teacher had instructed three or four of the bigger boys in the classroom to stay with her and physically restrain her from running out of the room. When I saw the family, the girl had been out of school for about three weeks. She was otherwise a bright girl whose schoolwork was good and who related rather well to the other children. The problem was simply that she was afraid of having her first period! She was eleven and had never been told about such happenings by her mother, but she had heard just enough from a girl in school to become petrified. Even at this, the parents wondered if telling her was right in a family session, or if it would do any harm. You might be interested to know that after two sessions, she was back in school.

The above example should not imply that the sexual problems of children and young adults are entirely the outgrowth of poor sexual education engendered by parental guilt, but it should be pointed out that when a parent is afraid of hurting a child by communicating sexual information, it says a great deal about the organization and dynamics of that family. And when this is true for the vast majority of families in our culture, we are all in trouble. It is not unlike the paradoxes in George Orwell's *1984*: hate is love, ignorance is knowledge, war is peace; when people learn what they should not, they double-think and that inhibits them. But when a sizable group of young people so vehemently reject the irrational rules and standards of their elders, we can all take a fresh look at ourselves and our values without those among us who chart new courses being branded as heretics or lunatics. If the young people have any single valid bit of evidence, what they are pushing is worthwhile. When we examine the extremely high incidence of sexual difficulty and inadequacy and pain in the majority of marriages in this country, certainly there must be better alternatives for what our past value orientations have produced.

The author now finds himself in what must surely be the same position of many who are over thirty. I have the intellectual capacities to see many absurdities in my own values and feelings, and I can understand my own perplexity and unsureness of sexual information when it comes to my own children. I do find it painful, however, to veer too far from the ways I was taught or, perhaps, the ways I was conditioned. Threatened by impending change, I am also envious of not being able to enjoy it. We may already be at a crucial point of choice. It may be that the family—as the social system which is responsible for the growth and emotional gratification of its members—as we know it, has so greatly invalidated itself that it will ultimately be replaced by other kinds of social organizations. We have already had a phenomenal growth in communal families. Only a short time ago, most of us did not know what a communal family was. Perhaps what Western culture now has to offer the world is its own version of the self-actualized individual: one who has freed himself from all the shackles of those parents who would use shame and guilt to motivate and control and who glides in and out of relationships on a here-and-now basis, seeking intimacy in the moment; one who is characterized by a sense of devotion to humanity, a spirit of adventure, experimenting in human relationships, conscious of the interdependence of persons on one another. Such young people would be quite a challenge to the traditional materialistic, achievement-orientated individual's past generations. However, this author is not so sure that the social system which creates such individuals can long endure. Nor can I be sure that the self-actualized individual who rejects the traditional family can favorably compete with a self-actualized family, one that has come to terms with its incongruities and hangups and recognizes the individual and emotional needs of its members and gives purpose to living. If the author had to bet on what was to be the dominant social system of the future, I would bet on the family; but the family is going to have to change. And if there is one area where it has suffered greatly, stifled its members, and irrationally hampered itself, it is in the sphere of sex. Perhaps with this book, we may get a better idea of what is wrong, where we are going, and what we can do.

2

First Nathan Ackerman
Memorial Address (1971)

Virginia Satir

This is the first time in my long association with Nathan Ackerman that he is absent at a meeting of this kind. I knew him long before there were many people in this field and there could be a meeting as large as this. I remember, for instance, back in the 50's going into hospitals and interviewing families and having the doctors and other people afterwards say to me in whispers, "I thought that myself but I could not say it openly." So, as I discuss these things now, I do not feel so lonely, and I do not think that Nat did later either; but there was a lot of loneliness for many years. I used to characterize myself as "working in the basement" and was naïve enough for a long time to think that no one knew what I was doing, but the process of osmosis is very interesting, and people knew more than I thought.

I did try to organize my thinking for this meeting, which I do not always do, and one of the things that I would like to do is to talk a little bit and then translate this into some kind of body pictures that relate to what we are doing as far as the family is concerned.

I like Thomas Weiss' definition of value, which appeared in a recent article. He said, "A value may be considered as a principle or a generalization that is preferred by some people in the conduct of their lives." Certainly if we look around today, we find that a lot of people look as though they are using different principles in the conduct of their lives. When I began writing this chapter, I was aware that I had been involved in a lot of these new things in the last five or six years, and I recognized that I was thinking about some of my own growth.

Twenty years ago, if someone had told me to get into a bath nude with some men, I would have turned pink and fainted. I do not know if there is anyone like that here now; there might be. When I thought of talking openly about sexual parts twenty-five years ago, I would have looked around for some scientific name. All I am saying at this point in time is that without knowing it, a lot of things have changed in me which no one taught me, but there was something in the atmosphere, I think, that helped bring this about.

In the first part, I shall review some things that I think reflect some of the changes we are talking about; ways in which we conduct our lives differently. I do believe that these are significant changes. . . . I would not want to delude myself, however, into thinking that the changes I see are by any means pervasive, because they are not. Along with some changes and parts opening up, there are other parts that are getting even more extreme and reactionary to those openings. So one end opens itself while the other end tightens, and we are working toward a kind of crisis in that sense.

For instance, I am very aware that today many newspapers, magazines, television and radio programs all reflect the ease of talking about things that have sexual import. I find a little more of it on the West Coast than I do on the East Coast, but nevertheless this is true throughout the country. We can use more of the language. "Fuck" is no longer a word that makes people drop dead; it may make them think sometimes. It reminds me that yesterday I had a letter from someone I presumed was a young psychology student who wanted to write a thesis on the implications of the "therapeutic fuck." (He had heard me make some comments in relation to it, and he was looking around for people he thought had some kind of status or something to see what he could get from them.) Now twenty years ago that would never have been talked about except maybe in very closed circles, although it may have been thought about. And certainly the relative ease with which books and movies that are concerned with pornography, nudity, and so on are available is relatively new. Today one can go into many big cities and see sexual movies without the same censorship as before. (This is by no means total, but it is certainly there.) Ed Lang, who has been in the forefront of the nude magazines, developed the Elysium Institute in Los Angeles, which I think is a pretty good one. A lot of the law, ordinances that relate to nudity, etc. have been either outlawed in the courts or stand a chance to be, so the context has reshaped itself in many ways. You are also aware that there is an increasing pressure to give sexual instruction, of a group sort, in the schools and not just of the birds-and-bees variety. That, too, has its counterpart reacting against it, but it nevertheless exists now. People are beginning to realize that there is a relationship between sexual knowledge and sexual pleasure and delight which was cut off for a long time. So in a way it is easier to say things now than it was before, and in a family, to be able to *really* talk and say anything out loud is possibly the beginning of making some new beliefs. You cannot get very far as long as you cannot talk openly and have to refer to a bull as a "gentleman cow." At least we have that going for us now!

I am reminded of a family I had worked with at one time in which no one had ever mentioned anything about sex. There were the usual questions, e.g. what will the children think if we talk about it? (I still get that from professionals). "Is it all right?" they ask, and I say, "People have been looking at it for a long time so I guess it's all right to talk about it." Out of this came a tape called "Care and Maintenance of the Genitals." It was a lovely name, but I could never keep it on my shelf. It was always being stolen, and unfortunately after making many copies, I do not have it anymore.

If we look again at another level, it is possible for students to think about having co-ed dorm life. And there is serious consideration in many quarters to giving the "pill" to fourteen and fifteen-year-olds and bringing up-to-date the fact that there is a relationship between the onset of menstruation and the ability to bear children; those two attitudes are getting a little closer together. There are also some changes going on in the abortion situation. This seems to me to have some relation to people being able to be in charge of themselves and to working toward more autonomy. I have always found it interesting that men were the ones who decided on abortion before, because they do not know anything about what goes on there at all!

There is also beginning to be in some quarters an interest in having deliveries at home, with the idea that this is a family affair. Children and fathers, as well as mothers, can then see the whole process. Years ago, I was one of the people who said, "Listen, since the father certainly is part of the whole birth process, he at least can feel himself more connected to it this way, because most of these connections occur in the dark . . . and so far in the past that they may be hard to connect with!" I used to think about the relative ease with which many men in our culture can leave their children, so I used to think that we could make more connections that way. Some of my doctor friends told me they do not like to do it because the men faint so much. I guess they will recover from that, but I do think it is useful to bring the whole process of birth and human be-ing into a perspective that one can look at.

Now there is another interesting development: An estimated two million people in the United States are active swingers. Swinging is where many couples, not just a few, get together to have sex. There is a good book with a preface by Martin Grotjan, which surprised but also pleased me, called *The Group Sex Tapes,* written by Rubenstein and Margolis. They interviewed a number of people in the swinging set. It is almost purely a sexual thing; however, most of the swingers still say that they really cannot go on with people too long unless they have some feeling for them. But they get together in groups to entertain and participate in all kinds of sex: oral, anal, anything they can find to do or which seems to be fitting at the moment. Rubenstein's study, if one calls it a study, seems to show that swinging is a liberating process. If people were hung-up just talking about things, swinging gave them freedom. There were many cases cited by the authors in which men overcame their impotence because their self-worth did not depend on their having an erection at that moment; someone else could come along and have an erection so that the woman would not be disappointed, and the man would not have to feel that he had failed.

There is another aspect which is very relevant to the family. That is that sexual exclusiveness is no longer the basis for intimacy between heterosexual partners. I think it has something to do with relaxation of ownership. ("I marry you so I own your penis.") Sexual exclusiveness can merely mean that I am validating my possession. By the way, they are still clipping the clitoris on women in parts of India and other places. Women do not wear chastity belts anymore, but there was a time when that happened. This whole business of gaining freedom from possessiveness has some relationship, it seems to be, to what swingers are trying to do.

There is serious talk going around some circles about the institution of marriage. Do we really need it? I believe it is hooked to the whole business of people wanting to get away from possessiveness in interrelationships. I often remind people that they do not have to be married to feel possessed by someone or to want to possess. It goes on between friends, in business, between parents and children. I think that possessiveness between people as a basis for a relationship is part of a self-worth problem and has very little to do with anything else.

There are also experimentations with different kinds of marriage forms: the communal marriage, group marriage where two couples get married, homosexual marriages. These are not always prominently displayed in the papers, but they exist. Some of you may remember a paper I presented before the American Psychological Association five years ago in which I labeled marriage as a "Five-Year Renewable Contract"; it is now published in *Family in Search of a Future*. I did not really mean that people should only stay married five years; what I was talking about was a kind of relationship where people could be free to be in love with each other. The interesting thing was the heavy mail I received for six months: "Communist go home." I must have had everything in the Bible clipped and sent to me. People were appalled that I was suggesting a deviation from the model of finding someone when you are twenty and sticking to him or her for the rest of your life, no matter how painful it might be. That was a sacrament of God. In a very real way, these sexual changes are now testing some of what we used to think were the sacraments. All of this, to me, adds up to more "cracks" in terms of where we were in the past. It makes it possible for us to think and feel openly about things that many of us thought and felt secretly about in the past. This does have an impact on the family, but when it comes to family therapy as such, it seems to me that the primary impact has to do with the therapist.

It is very hard to say that one ought to think this or that if you do not really feel it and think it yourself. There may be some therapists who with their heads believe that it is okay for young people to live with one another without being married, but it is not okay in their hearts or guts. When you think, how would I feel about my own daughter doing that, or my own son, somehow it comes out a little differently. Most of us at this conference are over thirty, and we have had plenty of time to get contaminated with lots of old ideas. So one of the difficulties is in looking at the changes in sexual attitudes and deciding how they fit for us. I think that all people who do any family therapy know that our words are only part of our whole message.

I was thinking the other day about what we are going to do with all the homes and services for babies born out of wedlock if we change our present ideas and accept it as natural to have a baby, married or unmarried, without stigma. I have a pair of professional friends who have lived together without marriage for ten years. Last year the woman had a baby and could not get the hospital to give that baby the father's name, even though he said he wanted it and that it was his. The hospital ignored this. So, again, we have not only our own attitudes but the attitudes of others to deal with.

There are also new ways of viewing behavior. For instance, twenty-five years ago if a man and woman came in for treatment and there was evidence of an extra-marital relationship going on, the tendency would be to jump to the conclusion that this was some kind of a neurotic expression. Now, maybe it is and maybe it is not. Maybe one of the things that happened is that we have asked people to behave in a way that is not human. Maybe people are like buildings and clothes in some sense; after a while, there is no more excitement in them. We have this tendency to repeat the same behavior but that may change with new values. The impact on the therapeutic endeavor is that we have to look anew. We may find out that what we formerly thought of as evidence of a neurosis is now, at this point, an effort of growth on the part of the individual.

This problem can be looked at in another way if we look at the whole family as a kind of system. I would like now to do some family sculpturing to bring this home to you. I am looking now through the eyes of the therapist; looking at a family in this day and age with some of these evolving kinds of changes and then asking, "What is the therapeutic job here?" I am going to put this "family" of four people in certain body positions that will come close to showing the way in which they might handle their communications. I am going to ask them to have a conversation about sex. These conditions reflect the communications and positions they might really have. I have just made them more extreme.

FIRST SCENE

The father is standing with his finger pointed at his kneeling daughter who is down on her knees and looks pitiful.

The son has a position similar to his father.

The mother has one hand on her heart and holds the other hand up.

Satir: Would you have a conversation about sex and tell your children about sex, please.

Father: One of the things you have to remember about sex is that when you go out with a boy, daughter, you make sure that he knows where you stand before you get in the back seat of that car.

(Silence)

Figure 2-1.

Mother: It is really nice that your father is talking to you like that. Maybe we should have these discussions more often. (Silence)

Son: Father is right, I would not want to go out with a girl who is loose. At least I would not want to marry her.

Girl: (Silent)

You notice they were not mentioning sex! We isolated forty-five different kinds of interactions and experiences of this sort, and I want to do a couple more. In examining it closely, the lead-out came from the way in which these people handled their communications. This had nothing to do with their inside, and if in addition you add ignorance, you begin to see something of what happens when perfectly intelligent people turn out like this. After a while, you can really see that this has nothing to do with sex; it has to do with who controls whom and under what conditions and with all the coalitions in the family; this, I found, was one of the things that happens when the word "sex" is mentioned. When I worked with couples who said, "I told my kids all about sex," I said, "Tell me what you told them."

They replied in the above manner. The family, like the one above, is split down the middle between males and females, dominating males and the submissive females. And later on the daughter identifies with her mother and marries a husband like her father, being a good student to the teachings of her mother.

SECOND SCENE

Figure 2-2.

Father is on his knees in a picture which one probably sees more often than that described above. This child has found out his parents are about to be divorced; the mother is not staying. He cannot make it in and cannot make it out. They are going to talk about sex now.

Mother: Why do you always come home so late?
Son: I didn't mean to. Somehow, all my friends kept me out.
Mother: Friends kept you out?
Father: What kind of friends do you have?
Son: Good friends.
Mother: A woman friend?
Son: Yes.
Mother: A girl or a woman!
Son: A little girl.

Mother to Father: Did you ever talk to him about women? You're his father.

The woman feels "Oh, how did it ever get to this point?" and feels sorry for her son. She is angry at her husband and has forgotten about her daughter.

The son feels scared, defensive, and is hiding his real thoughts behind guilt feelings. He is about eighteen-years-old and had a nice thing in the car with that "two-year-old" but "Oh my God, now what!"

The father felt he could not get satisfactory responses from either his wife or his son.

The daughter felt, "Thank God it is him this time and not me."

THIRD SCENE

Figure 2-3.

The third scene depicts "the democratic, reasonable family," particularly in the so-called middle-class.

They are all standing stiffly. The father has a noble look on his face and a prune look about his mouth. He acts as though his backbone is a piece of metal from the neck down to his fanny. They are talking about sex.

Father: Sex is the kind of thing we should talk about more often. Sex is beautiful.

One child: They are going to tell us about it in school next week.

Father: It brings people closer together.

Mother: Why don't we talk about it around the dinner table sometime?

Boy: I would like to talk about the kind of teachers they are going to have in that course.

Father: That is a good idea; we should talk about it.

Satir: Do you know when it will be done? Never.

The woman feels it was just a kind of polite talk with nothing in it.

The daughter was hoping that no one would ask her any direct questions about what was happening in school; and to be sure, no one will, not in this family.

The father felt that they were trying to disarm each other.

Changes in values do not mean anything, as far as positions in families go, as we have seen here. However, the subject itself and your reaction to it means something in terms of whether you as a therapist see into this kind of thing. Suppose you act like the last family members described above acted: "We are going to take a reasonable, objective attitude," which can happen. Again it comes down to the chance that the enlightenment that is present now can shape some new things, because I feel that the part of ourselves that has been so separated from our sexual parts or the rest of ourselves, as though it were something outside, is undergoing something new at this point. We are in a state of looking differently at many things, and for family therapists, the biggest job is how to utilize this new look for themselves so they are not continuing the same kind of processes that have been going on in the family.

Commentary: Samuel Granick

I think it would be useful to discuss some specific values in line with the theme of this seminar on the changing sex values in our culture. What are some of the values which are changing and how are they affecting the family?

One important area is the increasing openness with which sexual topics are discussed within the family setting. The frank presentation of the subject is no longer taboo for the newspapers, popular literature, or even the radio and TV, thus lending a cultural sanction to its consideration by family members. It is only a short step from this to the frank discussion between family members of their personal sexual problems and experiences. Indeed, within the family therapy setting it is now far from unusual for parental sexuality to be viewed as a family matter and to be shared with all of the family members.

Another value which has been changing with remarkable rapidity is the orientation toward virginity. Young people seem to be moving away from regarding it as a prized possession for both females and males. Thus, sex before and without marriage for both sexes is no longer frowned upon by a broad segment of the population. In point of fact, the view is now widespread that sex prior to marriage is quite helpful in enabling people to choose their mates wisely and maturely.

A significant change in attitude and behavior has also taken place with respect to pornography. It is no longer regarded as abnormal, or something to be ashamed of and kept hidden, to view frankly sexual films or read highly erotic literature. This kind of activity was previously regarded as sign of emotional disturbance and as a source of anti-social behavior. Now, however, the opposite seems to apply: It represents a satisfactory outlet for sexual tensions, a source of realistic information about sex, and is a help in achieving behavioral control.

The questions arises as to what effects these value changes

might have on the family. I perceive a number of ways in which these changes can be viewed optimistically. One of the important features is the sense of openness of communication which is promoted within the family, especially between the parents and their children. Sex is an area in which there are too often conspiracies of silence and avoidance between family members. Often the conspiracies show up as conflicts between the parents on one side and the children on the other. I am certain any one who has participated in family therapy has witnessed such conspiracies in the interactions among family members. When the opportunity is provided, however, to break through the sexual taboos and to communicate directly and honestly, this can go a long way toward integrating the family and facilitating open communication about other values and activities, such as social relations, educational and cultural matters, economic conditions and ethical conduct.

The nature of the value changes in the sexual sphere may also make it easier for family members to tune into each other's emotions and thoughts, thus creating a sense of mutual involvement, caring, and honesty of relating. I regard this as crucial in the development of a well-functioning family. It is the kind of orientation that enables parents to view their children as individuals and to encourage and guide them toward maturity and self-fulfillment. The children in such an atmosphere can feel secure in their dependency as they struggle toward independence. They can regard their parents as participants in the process of living and growing rather than as punitive and authoritarian agents.

Related to this is the possibility that children and parents may learn that the child-rearing experience is one which has much to teach all concerned about living and dealing with problems; that family conflicts and problems are most effectively handled when all participate. A comment I often find myself making to teenagers is that their parents actually have little or no training and experience for the complex task of raising them, and that growing up in the family is a cooperative endeavor, with each learning from and leading the other toward mutual understanding and empathic interactions. When the parents are helped to be aware of this, they usually relax a great deal and show less guilt and nervous tension about not having all the answers to the children's problems.

The open exploration of sexual and other taboo topics within the family also provides the parents with opportunities to demonstrate and share their values with the children, thus setting the stage for communicating with each other more often about important matters rather than mainly superficialities. It offers the children the chance to be open and honest toward the parents about their feelings and experiences.

When the home atmosphere is sympathetic, nonjudgmental, nonpunitive, and open, the way is clear for free and full expression of love, mutual concern, and supportiveness. Mutual dependency can then be accepted without guilt and anger and provide a basis for effective ego growth and strength.

A final point to be noted is that it is not a simple or easy matter to give up or change old values, even when these values are regarded as obsolete or of limited usefulness. The family sculpting exercise described elsewhere in this book demonstrated dramatically how each person tends to act in ways which are safe and comfortable for himself. We may thus expect considerable resistance in our family therapy sessions to the adoption of new sexual values and attitudes. With patience and support, however, we may be able to help parents and their children face realities, master their fears, and experiment with new orientations and ways of dealing with their sexual thoughts, feelings, and experiences.

It is possible to get carried away with what is new and often forget the virtue and value of the old. Questioning and resisting the "establishment" does not seem to prevent young people from consulting with us—the essentially "establishment" types. I doubt, however, whether we would be helpful or effective if we were to cling tenaciously and uncritically to old ways and attitudes. It behooves us to be in touch with the changing scene and with new developments in our field, such as the encounter and sensitivity awareness therapies. Experiencing them may help us achieve valuable changes in ourselves and enable us to be tuned into what the younger people are experiencing and communicating. At the same time we will be in an excellent position to evaluate the old and conserve what is relevant and useful in it. Particularly important would be our ability to interpret and apply the old wisdom in new contexts, thus maintaining continuity and communication between age groups.

Commentary: David Rubinstein

As a participant in this book, I want to comment on changing values of sex. Should I reveal how I have been changing? Should I discuss my own family's sanctions against talking about sex in public or even in the family? Should I describe my upbringing in a Latin American culture where joking about sex was proper among men but not among women? All these associations ran through my mind, but one particular story stayed with me like an obsessive thought, and it relates to the theme of this book, *Changing Sexual Values and the Family*.

A rabbi and his wife lived in a small town. Unfortunately, the rabbi died, and as so often happened in small towns, the other women of the town were responsible for the widow of the rabbi. The women had to make sure that she remarried; it just was not proper for a person of such stature to remain a widow. So the women got together to act as matchmakers. They found the widow a man, and after a proper courtship, they married. Off they went for the honeymoon while the women in the town wondered how any man could really match their departed rabbi. After the honeymoon, the women hurried to the new wife to ask what happened.

"Well, the first night was in between the High Holy Days, and I told him, 'Look, my departed husband, the rabbi, said that on these days you can not do anything.' But my new husband said, 'I have an uncle who used to be a rabbi, and *he* said that on these days it is allowed.' So we did it."

The new wife continued, "The next few night were the High Holy Days, very sacred, and I told my husband we still could not do it. He replied, "I had a grandfather who was very religious, and *he* told me it was allowed.' So we did it."

The story continued with more Holy Days and excuses and

23

more examples from new in-laws. Finally the new wife said to her friends, "I'll tell you, my new husband may not be as handsome or as wise as my departed husband, may he rest in peace, but I had so much fun with my new husband's relatives!"

This story kept popping into my head as I thought about changing values in the family and sex. One thought that came to mind is that sex as such is talked about in many confusing ways. We talk about the physical aspects of sex; sex as a way of intimacy; sex as discussion. Are we talking about the normal, healthy, desirable, warm way in which two people are as close as two people can ever be, or are we talking about physical encounters only? Are we talking about multiple affairs where a man must prove his masculinity or a woman her femininity? Which kind of sex are we discussing?

For centuries the family has tabooed the discussion of sex, and it may be possible that our culture has imposed that taboo for a purpose. Can we be as open about sex as we dream and fantasize? Should we talk about sexual intercourse in the presence of children in family therapy sessions? Very often sex in our family culture is still a secret aspect, protecting the intimacy that two people deserve to have.

We constantly experience stress over closeness, openness, and togetherness in counstling and in psycho-therapy. Is this stress really the result of striving for more closeness? It may be the result of the deep anxiety that occurs as we realize that we are only pretending to be close.

SWINGING

Commentary: Maury Levy*

Almost a dozen years ago, *Select Magazine* was started in South Jersey by a man named Frank Mason. He and his wife, Crystal, were swingers back when it was not too cool to talk about it. And they started keeping addresses and phone lists of their social friends, quietly circulating those handwritten lists for discreet parties. Eventually the list got some staples in it, then some ads, and pretty soon it became a whole magazine. Frank and Crystal Mason appeared a lot on the cover and hosted a number of parties, and that is how it all got going. And back then, the magazine was put together with rubberbands in a small back room by some very secretive people.

Today, it is all big business. *Select's* circulation is over 100,000. There are also other swingers' digests put out around Philadelphia now, but they are only imitators compared to *Select.*

Select's headquarters are now in the Select Building in Pennsauken's industrial park. It is full of paneled and carpeted offices, with receptionists, secretaries, mail sorters, an art department, and a computer room.

That is how Nelson Lynn, the current editor and publisher, got involved. He was a computer consultant who came in to organize things and ended up buying in and staying on. Nelson Lynn, though, is not his real name. Like many swingers, he prefers a pseudonym. This might say something about how far the movement still has to go.

Lynn has turned *Select* into a multi-million dollar operation. The revenue figures are overwhelming. *Select* is published six

* Swinging is becoming a significant social phenomenon. The following article is reprinted, with permission, from *Philadelphia Magazine* (August 1975) due to its relevance to Virginia Satir's presentation. —Editor

25

times a year and it usually sells out. The gross revenue from sales alone is over $2.3 million dollars.

An average 200-page edition of the magazine carries over 6,500 wide-ranging personal ads. Advertisements generate another $400,000 a year. Almost the same figure can be put on the money that comes in to forward the responses to ads. One never writes directly to one of *Select's* personals, but sends a response to a box number in Camden and, for a dollar or two, the *Select* people forward it. Add to this the revenue from the socials and the line of *Select* products, and a great deal of money is involved.

Nelson Lynn, who is still in his thirties, sits in his office and looks at his map of the United States, the one with all the little dots on it for each chapter of the World League of Swingers, his newest project, and he becomes very philosophical:

> As the Industrial Revolution moved around us, it became more difficult for each of us to live up to the traditional mating and marriage roles. Your needs get broader. And all this tends to create a pressure on the mating relationship which has caused swinging to come about as mostly a social, emotional and communications need much more than a sexual need.
>
> Sex is used as a hurdle. It becomes a trust item. In other words, if you can go to bed with my wife, or you can neck with my wife, or you can watch my wife and me make love, I share a trust with you. And that now means I can also tell you I can't afford that new car and confide other things that aren't sexual.

Lynn sees *Select* mostly as a service organization, a way of bringing people together. He says the new swingers are respected, fairly affluent family people. One demographic study he has shows that the "average" swinging couple has an income of $21,000 to $23,000; has been married seven years or more with two children and stable employment; are high achievers who are very conscious of looks and conditioning; that consume as many, if not more, goods than average.

That is where the swinging movement has really come out of the closet and become big business. Lloyd Levin, who works out of Chicago, is a marketing consultant to a number of major insurance companies. His specialty is new lifestyles and their marketability, and swinging is one of his major fields of interest.

Swinging is finally being accepted and studied, economically, by a lot of major companies. Levin says swingers now make up 5 percent of the population, and that the number is growing. "This isn't just a movement anymore," he says, "it's becoming an industry. And as the economy slips, people will become closer and closer together. And I think we're going to see a great surge in the extended family. And economic conditions are going to move us into swinging. The family unit just won't be able to stay the way it is. By the year 2000, it looks like we're going to have such a disproportion of men to women in this country, that it might be entirely necessary for us to legalize *polygamy*."

CHANGES

Commentary: Virginia Satir

I am trying to get at the impact of change on us because we are all products of the same thing. And what I can see in myself, in some of the presentations here on the family, and in some things in relation to my own daughters, is a big discrepancy.

I am thinking of what another therapist said to me about two years ago: "How about coming to a 'daisy chain' party?" A daisy chain party is really what swingers do. You get in a circle and you do a mouth-to-genital thing around the circle. I could not even think what that would be like! Yet I could encounter people who were thinking about it. And I was just going through the steps I personally had to take. To me, it was pleasing that I got to the point where I could actually see myself doing it—although I had not yet decided that I would. So one of the things I feel very good about in this meeting is that perhaps we can now talk about these kinds of things—with not only the mention of words—but also the images in relation to them.

I recently read an ad in a Berkeley paper which said: "Young male stud wishes companion. No responsibility requested. Everything open." I had a fantasy about answering that ad. So I took the steps, in my mind, and I could only go so far. . . . O.K., so I knock on the door and then I have to figure out how to make contact, to say, all right, let me try. As I imagined myself going to the door, what would be the first thing I would say? How would I feel?

The fact is that we are really examining our development. That is important but there is another thing, at least for me, and that is that people talk about behavior. I try to imagine how it could come out and how congruent it could be.

3

Family System and Society

MARGARET MEAD

BEFORE DISCUSSING THE family system in a changing world, I would like to address myself to some preliminary concepts. The principal scapegoat in society today is the middle class. Actually, the real point is not the middle class at all, but rather the fact that psychiatrists and social workers have always refused to pay any real attention to culture—middle class, upper class, lower class, black, yellow or red. This attitude, of course, has a lot of origins, one being the limited grasp of American life and culture held by many European leaders of psychiatry and psychoanalysis. They did, however, have a very high level grasp of psychoanalysis, and accustomed as they were to respond to *tones* of voice, they did not think that the language itself was very necessary. In fact, it took Franz Alexander about a year to reach the conclusion that a wealthy patient of his who went to an office on Wall Street every day when he did not have to, was not crazy, but was just acting like an American!

We have gone through a long period where nurses were taught that it was undemocratic to recognize that a patient was Italian, whereas in our V.A. hospitals (technically well-integrated for some time with a large number of black professionals), the real democracy of a staff conference was in not referring to a patient as "black" or asking a black professional to comment on a black patient. We have had some very peculiar situations as well, such as the Kansas farmer exposed for the first time to intellectual Jews from the Bronx—the devastation of these patients in Topeka is not less than it is for white middle class people who do not understand lower class Mexicans.

We had a very interesting case of a twelve-year-old boy in a residential home for children which was part of a state hospital system in Topeka. (We would have called him a "Negro" boy in those days; I am trying to be careful in my terminology to reflect the bias of each era accurately). About twelve years ago, television had decided to replay films of Belsen and Dachau, showing all the horror of concentration camps. Why twelve-year-olds in a treatment home were watching TV replays of films on Belsen is anyone's guess! This child's first therapist was a Hawaiian of Chinese origin. Since it was close to World War II, he thought his therapist was a "Jap," so his first few months of therapy were spent fighting the Japs. At the end of six months, due to our method of training child psychiatrists, this doctor was taken away from the boy and replaced by a new one. The new therapist was Jewish, *very* Jewish, and from New York City. Simultaneously, the concentration camp films were shown, and now the poor little boy had to deal with the fact that his therapist belonged to a group of people who had been subjected to all of those horrors. At this point, the boy gave up and joined the Russians. From then on, he represented the Russian army in any of his contacts with any therapist.

I think we have ignored the fact that we now have a new attack of guilt, that we are always specializing in some sort of guilt. We have decided that if we brand every type of insensitivity to other people as "middle class," then we can beat our breasts and beat everyone else under this heading. I do not think that this gets us very far. What we really need to do is to realize that therapists need to know something about the people they are working with, including the middle class. Many therapists are first-generation middle class, and therefore, do not know a thing about them. A great bulk of our school teachers are from the lower class, have just arrived in the middle class, and are holding on to it by their teeth. These teachers cannot tolerate lower class children because they interfere with their arrival in the middle class.

There is an even greater lack of understanding of the upper class by those in the fields of psychotherapy. A student I knew from the Philadelphia Main Line had a great deal of difficulty with a group of middle class professors. She called the professors by their first names, "Junior League" style, which did not please them, and she was also doing a thesis on touching people—which they did not care for at all. Only by threatening the professors with accusations of class prejudice, did I succeed in getting the student through.

In every field where the object of concern is an individual—psychotherapy, teaching, social work there is an enormous discontinuity of understanding. A New Englander trying to operate in Georgia does not do much better than if he were in Iran, as far as understanding what is going on. People who come from another part of this country and who we would consider to be part of our own class are nevertheless very alien. There are places in this country where it is considered a major insult not to invite your sister-in-law upstairs, if you live in a house with two stories, and families have actually broken up for life over it. Yet the same point will cause no concern whatsoever in many other places.

Increased techniques are needed for people to really understand something about the people with whom they are working—techniques which will give them the same background. By and large, there has been better understanding between psychiatrists and the poor or minority groups than with affluent patients. With the latter group you have all the taboo that you can never meet the other members of the family (a fascinating reversal of the FBI, who can meet everyone but the person they are investigating). Thus, the psychiatrist is left alone with the fantasies of his patient, uncorrected by reality. However, in a good deal of routine child guidance and family counselling over the past twenty-five years, there was a chance that the psychiatrist would know something about what was actually going on in a poor family, or one about to be evicted, or one in which someone had TB.

Before we go on with endless breast-beating and scapegoating about the middle class, there are a few assumptions that need to be corrected. I do not permit my students to use the word WASP. This shocks them since they only use it for derogating themselves and feel, therefore, that by saying "I am one of those awful WASPs" they are being rather noble. From my point of view, it is a word equivalent to "kike" or "nigger" and I consider it to be a straight denigration of a group by a negative stereotype.

Another important issue is the different rationalizations parents give for having children. The real reason they have children is because other people have children, and for no other reason. Whatever they say—whether they have children to worship their ancestors, to inherit the land, to work on the farm, for joy, to cement their marriage, for nice family lives—the fact remains that they have children because other people have children.

At present, I feel there are two points to be made about this. One is that we always expect good, Protestant self-respecting parents in the United States to lie to their children about how good they are. I cannot imagine anyone being brought up differently. Just imagine the father coming downstairs every morning and saying, "I didn't want to get up; I hate going to work; and I'm glad I'm late; I hate shaving; I kicked your mother in the belly last night." This is a fine way to get family life going! Parents are supposed to come down late for breakfast, to scold the children for being late, and if an impertinent child said, "You are often late, Daddy" he was told to keep quiet. On the whole, children had a much better image of their parents than was really true. When they were adolescents, they discovered their parents were not as good as this, but they believed somebody *could* be, so they had a nice ego-ideal to hand down to the next generation.

Now we tell parents they must only pretend to be as good or bad as they are, that it is wrong and dishonest for parents to pretend to have altruistic motives for having children. They are not to say: I am not going to make any demands on you and you are not going to have to support my old age; I did not bring you up to take care of the sheep and I did not have you to worship me when I am dead; I just had you because I thought it would be nice to have children.

I think we have to recognize that this is a style, and while we have broken the pretension and defenses of the past, we have not provided any new ones to work with. No matter what motives they may have started out with, most parents make enormous sacrifices for their children until they are grown. I think to the child who says, "You see, you only had me for your own self, you say you are altruistic and you love me and you bought this house out here so I would have lovely green grass and a nice school, but it was all for your own sake"—the parents can answer, "Well, on what terms would you have liked me to have you? To worship me after I am dead? To take care of the sheep? To form a nice band of brothers who could shoot another band of brothers and steal their sisters? Would you like that better?" Again we have a one-sided situation where people have very little comparative and historical sense, so we suddenly call all parents hypocrites.

We were all brought up to be hypocrites about sex until Kinsey. We had been promising our children that if they were good, they did not tell anyone they were having fun and did not have to feel guilty about it; but suddenly Kinsey broke that pact and published all those statistics. That was a real breach between society and the family; society failed to keep its agreement to continue to lie.

I also understand that some authorities have said that there is no generation gap. Most people who talk about the generation gap talk as if it were primarily a fight between youth and age or parents and children or professors and students, and that what we are talking about is adolescent rebellion. They think that the adolescents will grow up and get over it which I assure you, they will not.

We are talking about a particular breach between all the people who grew up before World War II and all those who grew up after it. The oldest of the people who grew up afterwards are now twenty-nine, and next year will be thirty. Ten years from now, they will be thirty-nine; in twenty years they will be forty-nine, and the generation gap will still be there because it is a gap between groups of people. In twenty years there will be grandfathers on one side of the gap and great-grandfathers on the other.

There are all kinds of conflicts between youth and age that go on in every society. There are particular ones going on now, as we are attempting to include young people in their own education and all sorts of other things. But these conflicts are not the "generation gap." The generation gap is something that happens once, and as far as we know, it would take something extraordinarily drastic to produce another gap of the same proportions as that produced by World War II, the bomb, space, the recognition of the population explosion, pollution and the electronic revolution, automation, and computers. All of this happened at once, separating irrevocably those who grew up before it from those who grew up with it. To create another generation gap of the same nature, something comparable to putting a colony on the moon and then blowing up the earth would have to occur. We would then have a generation gap between the people who lived on earth before they went to the moon and the kids born on the moon after the earth was blown up. (This is an explanatory fantasy, not a prophecy.)

This kind of gap is not only happening in America, it is happening in Japan, in Africa, in the Soviet Union, and everywhere in the world. There are always small generation gaps. When people first came to this country, within every immigrating generation from Europe there was a gap. The same was true of the people who first went to Australia. At the time of the Reformation, the fall of the Roman Empire, etc., there were again generation gaps for selected populations of one part of the globe. The unique difference now is that the present generation gap includes the whole world. The Second World War was such an experience that there is nowhere anyone can travel or no one who grew up and attained old age in this kind of world who escaped its impact. People who came to North America when it was a colony could go back to Europe, but they would recognize that children who grew up here knew something about living that their grandparents did not know: Here were people who woke up at night and heard the birds sing and knew what time it was. What is unique about this is that there have been a lot of generation gaps, but there has never been a point when the whole world became one and the world can only become one, once. Never before has man gone into space, nor has there ever been another World War II. These have coincided and been world-wide and so deep that they produced a different order of rift-a rift in *experience,* not in wisdom. Many people feel that if you say young people have had a different experience, it means they know more about *everything*. They do not know more about *everything*, but they know more about some things, and they look at everything differently. It is a break in perception.

At the moment, we have to recreate generation continuity. In the past, it had always been assumed that there was sufficient continuity of experience, if not between parents and children, then between someone else's parents and children, so that the teacher/therapist/statesman could draw on his own experience and appeal to other people. The older man could say, "Young man, I have been young, you have never been old." This is what society has been based on with a shift: Whenever there is great change, we find a lot of younger people doing a good proportion of the teaching. Never before have we had to recognize so great a difference in experience. Through human history, we have always been moving from the old to the young, from educated to less educated, from rich to poor, from powerful to less powerful—this has always been the style of life. Now we have a circular model, in which the old learn from the young just as the young learn from the old.

We used to educate the fourth-grade teacher, and she would teach the fourth grade for thirty years with a refresher course. A hundred years ago the teacher taught fourth grade better each year so that by the time she reached retirement, she had taught many people well. You cannot do this today because the children change. You cannot be a fourth-grade teacher or a family therapist, and follow the pattern that you learned when you learned to be a teacher or therapist without making changes. This is the principal reason we need the other generations, particularly grandparents and great-grandparents. Most people my age do know that something has changed, whereas people of forty think this is natural and cannot understand why other people do not recognize it.

A strange new kind of revolution is going on in this world today. There is nothing very new about the rebellion of oppressed or poor or enslaved people. This has been going on for thousands of years. Serfs and slaves and miners have been protesting against their conditions, and if they got strong enough to work on the conscience of those in power, they succeeded in eliminating the worse of those conditions.

What we are used to as a revolutionary style is people who have been abused and treated by badly intentioned people. That is, no one could claim that anyone enslaved the population for the population's good, however much theology was invented to rationalize it. No one ever claimed that a mine owner had a mine for the miner's sake! Everyone knew that mine owners have mines to make money and that miners worked in mines because they had no place else to work; they were herded into mining villages and did not even know there was anything else they could do. Eventually, labor leaders organized the miners to enforce better conditions, because these were people to whom evil had been done in the name of evil, such as love of money and so on. This is the kind of revolution we are used to.

Today the helping and the healing professions are facing something quite different. We are facing the rebellion of people unto whom we have tried to do good. We, as members of these professions, are also good. And the proof is that we are making less money for what we are doing than we could make doing something else. Of course, this is a fixed belief of the helping profession and may not be true of all psychiatrists. (Even so, it takes so long to be a psychiatrist and our expectation of life is so short that they can be forgiven.) As for the rest of the helping professions, we all know that we could make more as a janitor, street cleaner, or a typist on Wall Street. Everyone has given up a more lucrative profession for the noble and dedicated profession of helping people—even if this is not absolutely true, at least it is profoundly believed. Nevertheless, all the helping professions with the exception of a very few people in medicine have been badly paid and overworked, and they worked for the benefit of the people they helped. In spite of Lady Bountiful or middleclass morality or the rest of it, these people were climbing three and four and five flights of stairs doing things they believed were good for others. Teachers in this country have been underpaid and overworked, yet most of them cared about what they could do for their children; perhaps what they did was not wise or very good or very skilled, but those were their motivations.

There were some professors, a few for example, at the University of California, who apparently were making money elsewhere, but the bulk of college faculty in this country until the last few years were abominably paid and overworked. The only thing that kept us all going was nobility. Now suddenly, two things have happened. A lot of people—though still a relatively small number—have begun to be well paid. When you start a new program today, you may have to pay someone a living wage; even some of the charitable organizations now pay their secretaries a living wage. And you can even find a few social workers and teachers in New York City who are overpaid, so there are now enough who are well enough paid that people have begun to suspect that all of this is a career!

In the medical profession, we know how psychiatrists are treated and what the choice of psychiatry has meant in medical school. To have someone who wants to make money go into psychiatry instead of obstetrics is crazy. The place to make money is obviously obstetrics or neurosurgery—it used to be tonsillectomies—and specialties of this sort. Now we have a dedicated, poorly paid, noble profession, and the beneficiaries of their benevolent professional behavior are all rebelling, not because they have been done evil to, but because they have "been done good to"! This is new! The pupils who are being taught what they needed to know do not like it and they want to plan the curriculum. Students to whom the professor has given the same lecture every year for thirty years want to plan the curriculum and even want to elect the professors.

Welfare mothers demand the right to plan welfare programs and people feel that this really is the end! First we pay taxes to support them, and then we work so hard to give them all these things, and these ungrateful people want to have a part of the action too. Patients in mental hospitals also want a part of it. I think one of the most striking things I have heard was of a good Federal prison where one-third of the prisoners are in for smoking pot, one-third are conscientious objectors, and one-third are hardened criminals of one sort or another, and they all sit on a floor in an encounter session with the warden. This is what some people call "generation gap" in a sense, simply because it coincides with it. It is the college students who, after all, are on the other side of the generation gap from me. And it is the young school teachers who are just out of teachers' colleges, and young social workers in the agencies and the medical students who are on the other side of the generation gap who are taking this point of view; so it looks like the generation gap and partly so because they see things in a new way. It is also a very serious *re-evaluation of the position of beneficiary* and a terrible challenge, especially to people over forty, because they have given twenty years of their lives by now (that they can mention). Suddenly all the beneficiaries have rebelled, saying "We do not want to be done good to, we want to be part of the picture, we want to be in it."

I really do not know how to discuss the "family" in conflict with "society" because I do not know what "society" is, any more than I know who the "family" is. So I will have to translate this into my terms to make it a little more intelligible to myself.

In any society, there is a set of institutions—the family is one of them. It is a form in which we bring up children, regulate sexual rivalry, arrange who is going to feed whom, who is going to do the laundry, and to some extent, how property is to be transmitted, etc. Then we have government, industry, and the church as the other major institutional areas. For a long time, it was just the state, the church, and the family, in a sense, with continual readjustments as to who was going to do what. Whenever there was conquest by one country of another, it was quite likely that the education of the children, which had previously been done primarily in the family, would be taken over by the state. If you want people to speak a language other than their mother tongue, then you cannot learn it from mother. So, the state took education out of the home, although with people of the same social level somewhere else, a good deal of education would go on in the home. Industry has really been added in the last hundred years as a major factor. To a degree, these sets of institutional patterns are always working for some kind of balance of power. Each group tries to get the other governmental group to do the things they cannot do well.

One of the outstanding things in this country is the way in which people with religious morality, which is relatively unrelated to the core of their religion usually but is temporal and temporary, try to make the state make their parishioners behave. This is the entire history of attitudes in this country toward abortions, birth control, divorce, blue laws, Sunday opening, gambling, drinking, and drugs. The religious constituency which was interested in a certain point has never been strong enough to make its own people behave, so it got the state to pass a law for all of the people. Thus it was the extraordinarily strong Protestant ethic backing up such things as Prohibition in the Prohibition era, and it was primarily the strong Catholic constituency (mostly rural, originally) that wanted the state to pass laws about abortion and contraceptives because it could not keep its own parishioners in order. On the other hand, whenever the state interferes with something in the church that annoys the state, the church immediately insists upon its autonomy from the state and is accountable only to Almighty God and no one else!

However, the families in our society—with the exception of the Mafia—are not organized the same way as the state, the church, and industry. The Mafia are groups of *organized* families who put family loyalty and family discipline above the state; they invented this when Sicily was a conquered country, giving them a lot of practice which they put to other uses.

China, for hundreds of years, has been a country in which

the family was the strongest institution. The family might have 2,000 people in it, but loyalty to the family, discipline, and counsel remained within the family—no one would ever have gone out of the family in classical China to consult a psychiatrist. They had their own Council inside which would have been a little different, but there were people that you could consult there; however, loyalty and morality belonged to the family and not to the state. The state was thoroughly corrupt, and the families knew how to keep judges in order. One of the results of the communist revolution in China has been an attempt to shift from family loyalty to national loyalty. But in a country like ancient China, you really could see the family standing against the state. Since there was no organized religion whatsoever, it was primarily the family and the state who were concerned with what was going on.

Now in our style of life, it is important to realize that "the family" has no spokesman. Until the present consolidation of HEW, it did not even have a proper voice within the Federal structure except in the Department of Agriculture. In the 1930's, there was a marvelously unified approach to life in the Department of Agriculture, the kind of thing we are trying to do now by taking twenty professions and fastening them together. The Department of Agriculture was responsible for all people who lived in communities of 2,500 or less from the cradle to the grave—their nutrition, their family organization, their dependencies, their education—and this is one reason why so many things were right with the Department of Agriculture. But even the Department of Agriculture did not have real responsibility for the family. I remember going to an exhibit by the Bureau of Home Economics in West Virginia which was filled with model kitchens circa 1945 or '46. There were kitchens where the only place a baby could fit in was under the icebox. There was not even any place to suspend the baby from the ceiling! When I looked at these model kitchens, I wondered, "Where do you put the baby?" They said "But you see, there is no department of family life in the Bureau of Home Economics in the Department of Agriculture." You see, we are not very much further today.

In 1949, we did have a national conference on "the family" and it became a respectable term; people could quote things we were saying about it and states then had something to talk about concerning family programs. But actually, there is no voice for the institution of The Family, so it gets handled in a variety of ways. If you want to protect the family by having stringent divorce laws, then the religious groups come forth and try to interfere with the private lives of other people in the name of supporting the family. Theoretically, HEW is supposed to deal with the rest of the country that does not include Agriculture, but there is no central spot where someone looks into everything that is happening to affect family life in this country. As a result, things can shift back and forth very rapidly.

In the early 1940's, Lawrence K. Frank, who was one of the great pioneers of the kind of thinking we are trying to do here, talked about the fact that the family subsidized every other institution in the country. The family took up the slack when the schools, which are part of the state, failed. The family nursed the sick, dealt with the people who had been crippled in industry, and took care of the aged whom industry and the state did not provide for. In fact, we expected the family to be primarily the institution which took on all of the vicissitudes of society.

By 1955, the whole apparatus of the country was serving the family. It was constructed so that everyone who wanted to could have a house in the suburbs as rapidly as possible with a thirty-year mortgage on it. Industry was pleading with its employees to accept promotions and they would go home and "talk it over with the family." And the families would say, "No, daddy, we want you for picnics," so a third of them would not accept promotion at all in the 1950's—thus, things were heavily focused around the visible family. The visible family was the family that lived in the suburbs or could afford to move to the suburbs. Virtually every single kind of legislation in the country—the way we handled veterans' benefits, the way we handled annual housing loans, the available resources that came from the Federal Government for housing—all went into housing suburban families. Meanwhile, of course, life in the inner cities and life in the rural regions went to pieces. There was the ideal family in a station wagon; five children, a dog and a cat, who lived in the suburbs and had a minimal relationship with anyone else. This dominated advertising, clothes, employment, educational styles, everything. It was a period of low-level goodness.

The 50's were a very good and innocent period. There were no demonstrations, only panty raids. Drug abuse had not yet appreciably started, it was reasonably confined to minority groups where no one really cared except to pass laws to punish them if necessary. It was a period where family life was crucial and was the value this country was running after with a tremendous disregard for anyone who did not have the economic resources to produce that kind of family life. As this was pretty well established by the early 1950's, most people today think that was the American Family, so we hear a great deal of talk about the modern family falling to pieces: This is the end of the family, or if there are young people who want to live in groups, this means the end of family life. It reminds me of a cousin of my mother's who said to me in 1917, "You know, if your mother were getting married today, you know what she would have done? She would have kept her own name. Do you know that when Fred and I got married, your mother thought we could form a cooperating household of two couples. Think of it, two couples!" And then she said, "Furthermore, your mother was always talking about cooperative laundries!"

Now we have had the ebb and flow, back and forth, between families that were related to other people—the people who married and lived near home and had large numbers of relatives around—and between different ethnic families in this country. At the same time, we have glorified as the American Family the isolated suburban family with no one else to depend on. The good family is always totally independent and needs no help from any agencies. Of course, we relieve their shame and guilt if they have to have some help and try to tell them that "the best people" need help. But we do not believe it. We believe in the family where the father is able to support the family in a continuing state of affluence, where they never need any help from anyone, where they can hire a private pediatrician, and move to a suburb that has good schools and keeps everyone else out and votes against the bond issue. This is the family we have been glorifying plus something that has never been true in this country before, a family that kicks its adolescent girls out as soon as possible.

Fifty years ago, there was room for a daughter in the kitchen; then they built a kitchen where there is no room for another woman. Servants disappeared, aunts disappeared, grandmothers disappeared, and we built a kitchen with an icebox and a woman who could not bear to have another woman near her. The bulk of young mothers today grew up in a household which was made up of small children, one woman, one man, and a babysitter. We turned in-laws into babysitters and then as they came in, the parents could go out and never had to see them. A few people had a cleaning woman and when she came in, you went out; thus we raised a generation of women who cannot tolerate another woman in the same household. At the same time, the age of puberty is dropping four months a decade. We are beginning to throw our daughters out at eleven or twelve now. The minute they begin to look like women, in this kitchen, they bump into each other. The kitchens are not organized for two people with any protuberances. So, beginning in the 50's, we began forcing girls into pregnancy and marriage—the entire maternal apparatus of this country was trying to get the girls married and, if necessary, pregnant to get them out of the home. We organized the style of life which meant that a boy and girl went from dependency in one home straight into marriage with no experience whatsoever (if you could not afford to get away to college, or go away for the experiment of international living in the summer). Some girls managed to get through college before getting married, and they had to live at home until the mother pushed them out.

This was our standard family . . . and I hope it is going to pieces. But I also think we have to recognize that the nuclear family—named before the bomb—is an extremely unnatural family. Throughout human history it has never been natural to send a pair of young inexperienced parents with little children out into the world all by themselves with no older people to advise and help them pick up the pieces. However, this country was founded by the nuclear family; it was the ideal family for very rapid, drastic social change. If an enterprising young man could find a tough enough and enterprising young girl, they picked themselves up and crossed the Atlantic. They left the old people where they were and they established this as a style. When the older people got here, people picked themselves up in Maine and Vermont and went West. On the whole, the more timid girls stayed home and kept the men they could keep home with them; this gave a special style to the village, since the enterprising left and the less enterprising stayed. We know that the best way to colonize is to send out a young unmarried couple without children. They are committed to each other, they at least have each other in a new situation, and they have no children yet to make them cautious and conservative and frightened. But if you want to explore, you send men alone, and then you know they will come back. On the whole, you do not send middle-aged people as colonists.

Today in India, the nuclear family is the ideal way for a man to educate his daughters. They go to Karachi or Bombay, get away from the villagers, and live the way they want to live. Thus you can see that the spreading form of family has been fostered by rapid social change and the need for each generation to make a style of its own—even where the elders were adamantly against the new life style.

What are we trying to do in this country, with all the turmoil about the present styles of family life? The styles are bad and the people are victims, in many instances, because the grounds on which both girls and boys married are unsupportable today. A large number of settled families are too committed to change very much, but they have to learn to live within the pattern they have. As I see it, what the younger people are trying to insist upon is that we need a larger community. We probably will never again have an extended family of thirty or forty biologically related people living near each other. It is just as well, because most people who idealize the village have never lived in one; if they were born in one, they go back once a

year, forgetting that if people live with the same people generation after generation, they accumulate hate. It is reasonably
doubtful that they accumulate love, although they may accumulate loyalty or a deep habituation to that environment, but all
the grievances pass down from one generation to another. Every
time I went to visit my cousin Mary, my mother said, "Did
you see those forks that belonged to your great-uncle which
should have come to me?" (I have another friend who has
beautiful coffee spoons, the ends of which were chopped off so,
as to divide them up equally).

What I believe will happen is going to take a lot of work, a
lot of imagination and a lot of innovation. It demands entire
town planning and housing which will make it possible for
groups of people to live together; it is open-ended, so when an
IBM computer transfers someone to another part of the country,
someone else can come in. But the planners must have sufficient
agreement on life style so that they provide the things that used
to be provided before we developed the nuclear family. Then
there were enough people of a similar kind to give children
security and a variety of models, which are two very serious things
that are lacking in the nuclear family of today.

The major point here is that we have to revise the community
style we have been building for twenty-five years (and in
Philadelphia a little longer), which essentially saw an unviable
form of life as the good life. That is the notion of living in a
community where all people are about the same class, same
age, same religion—so all nice people have the same nice
standards wherever they work, live in autonomous little houses
with a little bit of green lawn and enough hardware to run a
Roman palace, in a community in which each family is responsible
for itself and independent. This picture of community life is
bad, and we are going to have to redesign it in ways that make
it possible for all sorts of changes. For example, there ought to
be greater density, so people are closer together, because one
of the great harms of suburban life is the distance from anyone
you know; communities where people of different ages can
live together so that you do have one of these blocks with
forty-three tricycles on the sidewalk; houses of different sizes,

different shapes, different economic levels, so that we can bring up our children to live in a world with people of different ages and races and classes and prevent the kind of clashes that come when there is a barrier or line between one economic group and another, as we have at present. Obviously, these will not be built overnight. There is a limited amount of good real estate available, and there are few apartments left that were built in the 20's containing little and big apartments where you could put grandmother on the tenth floor and a large family on the second. This is the sort of thing that Puerto Ricans usually look for in New York City so that different related people can be near each other, but there are not many of these buildings, although there still are brownstones where three or four houses are put together.

Building these communities takes a great deal of imagination and is mainly going to be done by very active, energetic and ideologically motivated people. So I think one has to think of less satisfactory substitutes to the extent that we group people supporting families in groups that are relevant to them. There is a great difference between an old suburb where there were adequate social groups into which the newcomers could be accepted and the new suburb where families do not know each other at all, or the new slum area where they keep moving and running away from the landlords and the rats to the point that there are no centers. I believe we have to recognize that what families need are other families. This is the terrible point made a few years ago when two sociologists who had studied families advised every family to stay away from every family that had a problem, including a family that had been broken by death. What we need instead are communities where the different needs of different families make it possible for each family to help the other in some way. Unless we build this kind of community structure, I think that family therapy will not accomplish what it should.

Commentary: Mel Roman*

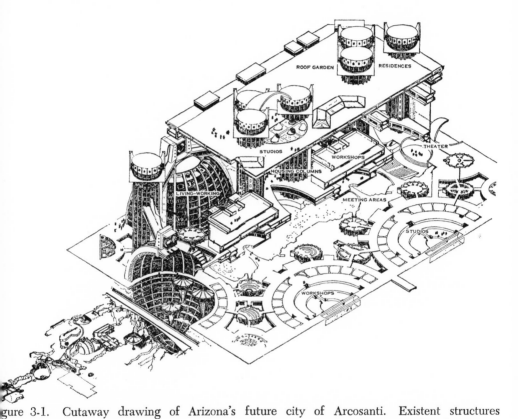

gure 3-1. Cutaway drawing of Arizona's future city of Arcosanti. Existent structures
ar left) serve as urban study center for psychiatrists and other experts. This drawing is
printed from the book *Arcology, The City in the Image of Man* by Paolo Soleri with the
mission of MIT Press.

In the Arizona Desert a vertical city called Arcosanti is under
construction. It will accommodate 3,000 people on a nine acre

* The following comments have been published in *Frontiers of Psychiatry*,
January 15, 1974, Volume 4, No. 2. They are abstracted and reprinted here,
with permission, due to their relevance to Dr. Mead's statements about living
arrangements in the city.

site. Conceived as a single modular structure, thirty stories high, it will contain all living, working, learning, leisure and support-system space required by its citizens.

Someday Arcosanti may be dwarfed by Hexahedron, a city twice as high as the Empire State Building, standing on 140 acres, with a population of approximately 120,000—about the same as Savannah, Georgia. Helping to plan such habitats of the future, with specially designed mental health-care delivery systems, is an exciting challenge to practical visionaries on frontiers of mental health sciences.

Arcosanti and Hexahedron are the brainchildren of Italian-born futuristic architect and "urban prophet" Paolo Soleri. His bold conception of tomorrow's cities is attracting great interest among experts who believe that today's chaotic, corrosive urban environments pose severe threats to man's psychological and material well-being, not to mention survival.

Soleri's radical concept of tomorrow's city emanates from his concern over the estrangement of today's city dwellers not only from other classes but also from their own families and friends. Indeed, the entire field of futurist speculation and activity that is Soleri's milieu has strong mental-health implications.

Futurism is an attempt to understand contemporary problems by looking to the future rather than the past for illumination. Based on the belief that the future is ours to create, it recognizes, as the author of *Future Shock,* Alvin Toffler,[1] stated, that "every society faces not merely a succession of probable futures but an array of possible futures and conflict over preferable futures." Futurists wish to convert certain possibles into probables, in pursuit of agreed-on preferables.

Most futurist studies are speculative, but they are not irresponsible. Many psychiatrists, and other experts as well, have noted that individuals are presently suffering from an inability to keep pace with the rate of change in our society. So, when mental health professionals try to assess where they are and where they are going—as many are now beginning to do in the face of our approaching National Bicentennial—they find they just cannot get a solid fix.

This results in *future shock*, a kind of symptom complex of alienation, hopelessness and confusion, leading often to denial and avoidance of the change that is taking place. Governments, as well as mental health-care institutions, suffer from a kind of collective future shock, a breakdown of their decisional processes. One cannot live in a society that is out of control, as chaos breeds illness. There seems to be a need to assume some kind of control over change. Conventional planning is too short-range. Stewart Updall made this point by saying that problem solving can be risky, for the tendency is to isolate the problem. Indeed, to the extent that our technology succeeds so well in providing solutions to problems—air-conditioning the individual apartment in a city choked by pollution, for example—Soleri is wary of technology. Piecemeal approaches to mental health-care planning are equally disastrous.

The community mental health movement provides a basis for getting involved in the kinds of broad speculative issues involved in futurism. The CMHCs are reconceptualizing their activities away from a strict medical model and toward a quality of life model with an emphasis on prevention: The logical next step is toward promotion of mental health, not just prevention. This means providing possibilities for greater personal growth. However, mental-health professionals need to concern themselves with society's direction over and above what they can accomplish through the CMHCs, and soon. Apart from mental health promotion, this is particularly an urgent matter in the context of the M.I.T. study, "The Limits to Growth," which predicts the most dire consequences for the life-support systems of this planet beginning within the next forty years if society continues along its present course.

Soleri is convinced that the fate of man rests with the cities, with their highly complex, interactive life-styles. Also, he believes that as there is a discipline in our body, so the body of society has to have discipline: that is, the ability to be highly complex. It is within this complexity that the individual elements are going to be able, through the intensity of connection, to develop their own personal freedom. Life has evolved biologically: Now it is evolving technologically, but the goal seems to be that life has to become spiritually more intense.

At the same time, Soleri enjoys nature and the outdoors. Suburbs do not reconcile these poles, Soleri argues, since they tend to segregate people by time and distance. They encourage further outward expansion, so that those dwelling in the middle reaches of suburbia become separated from nature as well as from the cultural institutions of the city.

Soleri proposes the building of vertical cities. He calls them *arcologies,* architecture plus ecology. Home dwellings are located on the skin of the city, public facilities at the core. Thus, citizens have two views: one of land and sky, the other of the interior landscape. This interior, for Soleri, is not separate from nature: Rather, it constitutes a kind of man-made nature that exists on a continuum with mother nature. The design reflects this concept: Arcologies are multilayered, with porches and patios jutting out to admit different kinds of light. The 30th floor might be a lake.

Soleri and others firmly believe that the technology necessary for such a development exists. The Hancock building in Chicago, while by no means an arcology, is a 100-story structure that provides both living and working space. And Co-op City in the Bronx is a high-rise complex for 60,000 people. The Co-op City undoubtedly has become anonymous and unhealthy, with all the symptoms of beginning crime, transportation difficulties, inadequate planning for health services. It is ugly, but it does not have to be so. Soleri believes that density in itself does not have to be negative. He thinks crowding is a very positive thing.

Oscar Newman's *Defensible Space*[2] is an attack on the security issue involved in high-rise buildings. Such failures have been used as bad arguments against Soleri's cities. Soleri's high-density habitats are vital, colorful environments where space is alive with rich human interaction. Co-op's spaces, in contrast, are private and segregated. As far as segregation is concerned, Co-op has a superhighway dividing it right down the middle.

Segregation, as it affects mental health, is one of Soleri's major concerns. This is an important point as people tend to segregate themselves physically and psychologically. If one works in one place and lives in another, he is already splitting his psychic life. The price is a loss of the sense of his life being one fabric: One begins to develop different social networks. Soleri's remedy is to integrate living and working spaces.

There should be no illusions about conflict being absent in an arcology, but it is possible to have a joyful community life "with conflict." As for rat studies demonstrating the ill-effects of crowding, one should say, people are not rats. Further, most of the present studies in density and conflict are unconvincing. It is an area of research which one hopes will be pursued more vigorously. Certainly, high-density centers vary. Hong Kong, for example, has very high density without any apparent detrimental effects. Livability seems to depend on the degree of community purpose and coherence.

The author is inclined to say that he agrees with the editor of *Design and Environment*,[3] who wrote, "We have no idea of the sociological or psychological consequences of populations concentrated to the degree that Soleri's arcologies envision." It is true. More psychiatrists and behavioral scientists should get involved in such studies. Soleri's response to the criticism that arcologies impose a particular social structure that amount to totalitarianism is that he never advocates a social system because he is not able to define one. He is advocating a landscape for a social system. And this landscape, for the moment, is what the earth gives us. His contention is that this landscape is not sufficient any more because we are too complex, as individuals, as society and as a civilization.

In other words, Soleri is merely providing a physical container within which human aspirations can have free play within essential, and desirable disciplines.

An arcology does not imply a collectivist society. Divergent life-styles would be encouraged. A traditional family might neighbor on a commune. The dwellings in the outer skin are not conceived as beehives, but spaces that could accommodate anything from a small house to a tent.

There would be no ideology to preserve, so there is no analogy to the Soviet Union. The culture of the arcology would simply become what its residents make of it. While the role of the mental-health professional would stay essentially the same, it is likely that the delivery of health-care services would be easier. High-speed elevators and less cluttered pedestrian byways would facilitate travel to any part of the city in thirty minutes or less.

Aristotle's prescription, that no city should have a circumference exceeding that in which a cry for help, wherever uttered, can be clearly heard at the outer gates, has obvious relevance to Soleri's "miniaturized" cities and immediate appeal to those of us in the community mental-health movement.

REFERENCES

1. Toffler, Alvin: *Future Shock.* Random House, 1970.
2. Newman, Oscar: *Defensible Space.* "Crime Prevention Through Urban Design." McMillian, 1972.
3. Ferebee, Ann: *Design and Environment,* Volume 4, 1973.

4

Sexual Problems in
Marital Therapy*

JAMES L. FRAMO

SEXUAL PROBLEMS HAVE traditionally been classified and treated as conditions or illnesses existing within an individual. These problems have been broken down classically into such topics as impotence, frigidity, premature ejaculation, and perversions, and the emphasis has been on individual treatment. As we now know from family and marital therapy, behavior does not occur in a vacuum. Symptoms are by-products of relationship struggles, and they occur in a context; most symptoms, including sexual symptoms, are formed, selected, faked, exchanged, maintained, and reduced as a function of the intimate system in which they are embedded. Note that I do not say (as do some family therapists) that intrapsychic forces are unimportant. Neither the intrapsychic nor transactional levels can be replaced by the other or reduced to the other; I believe both are necessary for the whole picture. The enormous complexity of the relationship between the two levels has only begun to be explored, and it will take a super-Freud someday to give us that kind of breakthrough.

In this study I will approach the subject of sexual problems largely from an interactional perspective, since I treat couples together. If I stress the interactional over the intrapsychic, it is only because I want to highlight the crucial importance of a perspective that has been so neglected. I agree with Carl

---

* A different version of this paper was published in the *Journal of Medical Aspects of Human Sexuality* under a different title. This paper is printed here with permission of Hospital Publications, Inc. All rights are reserved.

Whitaker that when a marriage is in serious trouble the likelihood of divorce is much greater if the partners go to two therapists separately or if only one goes for treatment. At any rate, I would like to discuss some of my clinical experiences in treating a variety of sexual problems as they appear in marriage therapy (incidentally, not all the couples I see are formally married). Some of these topics are loaded and are likely to give rise to anxiety. The disassembling of an experience into concrete terms has much greater impact than stating the experience in the abstract. It is one thing for a wife to say, "Darling, I've had an affair," and it is quite another sort of thing for her to go into detail or give particulars.

In this report I will make some comments on marriage in general and on its viability in our society. I will discuss briefly some of the dynamics of relationships in marriage and about the role of sex in marriage. I will be discussing disclosures of extramarital affairs in couple therapy, the range of reactions of the mates to the disclosure, and subsequent effects on the marriage relationship. Sexual myths and professional myths will be mentioned, as well as some of the interpersonal by-play and marital games surrounding impotence and frigidity. And finally, I will discuss some of my treatment methods—all the way from work with the couple as a unit, through involvement with the family of origin, couples learning to deal with the issues between them, techniques for making an empty relationship more exciting, for couples group therapy, and "divorce therapy."

In these observations about deeply personal issues which are so intertwined with values, I will try to be as objective as possible and report things as I have seen them. It is, of course, impossible to be totally value-free in psychotherapy.

As everyone knows, there have been more social changes in the last few decades than at any time in our history—more women working since World War II, the black revolution, the demoralization of the country over Vietnam, large cities dying and the exodus to suburbs, Women's Liberation, the emergence of a highly technological society, the drug culture, the so-called sexual revolution, etc. The clinician, of course, finds manifestations of these social and cultural movements in his practice, especially in marital and family therapy. There is, for instance, the example of the older woman who said, "What a fool I was to hold onto my precious virginity before I got married; these young kids today have the right idea." The effects of changing values—especially sexual values—as they have affected the marriage relationships I have seen in my office will be noticeable in many of my observations.

At this point I must make a few comments about marriage in general. I am not dealing with the deeper dynamics here, but with some rather startling statistics and observations. In a recent study by a lawyer, who examined the statistics carefully, it was found that the true statistics of the divorce rate in this country are that 50 per cent of marriages now end up in divorce. In some parts of the country, such as suburban Los Angeles, the divorce rate exceeds the marriage rate. Considering that this statistic does not take into account the number of married people who stay together unhappily, we can understand why some people question the viability of marriage as a social institution! It also makes understandable the experimentation going on today with the varieties of group and multiperson marriages. (These other forms of "marriages" have their own complicated difficulties, but that is not the focus of this discussion.) The skepticism and cynicism with which today's youth view traditional marriage is an important trend with powerful implications. I hear over and over the statement, "When I look around me at all the marriages I know, I can't think of one couple I'd say is really happy; you certainly can't tell how a marriage is doing by how the couple behaves publicly; when you get to know people well you find out how bad the marriage really is." It is true, in a sense, that the public reports given out about one's marriage are like the communiqués issued by the heads of state after a meeting—neither one tells you very much about what's really going on. But I believe that a realistic view of marriage, based on intimate knowledge of a couple, has to recognize not only the cliché that all marriages have problems, but that in the course of a marriage over time, *every* marriage has *serious* difficulties to the point where divorce is at least considered. (The difficulties, it is true, may be disguised as emotional or physical distance or by "pseudo-mutual" relationships.) All of this confirms the observation that of all the conceivable kinds of human relationships that exist, the marriage relationship is the most difficult to work out and requires the highest level of maturity. It is easier, for example, to be a parent than it is to be a mate.

A more balanced view of marriage is not as pessimistic as the foregoing suggests. Individuals in the helping professions are in danger of developing a distorted view of human relationships because when people come for help they are seen at their worst. I am aware that there are many positive sides to marriage relationships that do not appear in the treatment room.

One of the most important things that happens in marital therapy is a sorting out of unrealistic expectations, the lowering of some expectations, and the raising of others. Because of conflicts handing over from the family of origin, many people are unable to make an emotional commitment to the mate, other than fantasies of romantic fusion. Many married persons' primary commitments and loyalties are to the parents rather than to the mate; this, as I see it, is one of the primary causes of marital problems. If the partners are able to differentiate from the family of origin and from the intermeshing of the marital symbiosis—that is, become more separate as persons— not only do expectations become more realistic but the partners even stop searching for "happiness"—which is, after all, a by-product of other things and not a goal in itself. I remember Harold Searles saying something once that sounded jarring at the time but now makes sense. He said: "Unless my wife and I can live without each other we cannot love each other." This statement, of course, does not jibe with the popular mystique propagated by ladies' magazines that "togetherness" is the ultimate bliss (I might mention that attempts to achieve inner differentiation by external means can take the form of precipitous divorce. In these cases the therapist has to examine just whom the person is really getting divorced from; the rejected mate is often a stand-in for an internal object derived from the parents). On the topic of remarriage, incidentally, we are all familiar with the person who searches for happiness in one marriage after the other. One patient in his seventh marriage said that his first marriage was probably the best and offered the best chance for working things out. To be sure, some second marriages do work out better; one explanation for this is that the person splits the ambivalence, leaves the hatred toward a parent with the first mate, and is then free to love the second mate. In the enmeshed symbiotic couple, part of each individual's psychology is fused with the other's—which is one of the reasons many desperately unhappy married people cannot leave each other. Some partners, however, are so separate that they are truly disconnected from each other; many of these people are unable to be married, and I do not think society should pressure all people to be married.

Returning to the topic of sexual problems, it seems to me that at least some of the problems were created by professionals who wrote sex manuals which set standards for sexual performance that few people could meet, especially men. All kinds of mythologies were created. One can be seen in the couple who came to see me because they were not having simultaneous orgasms all the time. If you have read a lot of those sex manuals, they make sex sound like hard work; all the fun and spontaneity are lost. In addition, most of them were addressed to men on how to arouse their "passively receptive" wives; they must control themselves and think about baseball until the wives are ready. I have seen more men who talk about how exhausted they became trying to follow the books! (One fellow got so tired stimulating his wife that he used an artificial penis in order to ward off his wife's complaint that he could not satisfy her.) Some couples, emphasizing performance, spend hours going for sexual records, and these marathons, since they are often basically frantic efforts to recapture past romance or to save a dying marriage, rather than being fulfilling are more like athletic contests. Some of the Masters & Johnson techniques, which take the stress off performance, and slow down love-making so that caressing, touching, kissing and petting can have the excitement it did during courtship, can be very useful. (Women's Lib might be interested in this case: We are all familiar with the complaint of some women that they are treated as sex objects;

one husband I saw told of how *he* felt treated as a sex object, and exploration revealed that his wife's mother sent his wife every new sex manual; he was expected to try a different technique every time. It will come as no surprise that when I saw this couple they had not had sex relations for the previous year.) I think the book *The Sensuous Woman* is a healthy antidote to all the books directed to men, although with those couples who have been reading a lot of books on sex instruction (without anything changing in their sexual relationship), I usually suggest they get rid of the books. I do believe that Masters & Johnson have done a lot to dispel many sexual myths which were creating such havoc. What a relief it is for couples to discover that there is no essential difference between a clitoral and vaginal orgasm! I often have to do some straight educating on sexual matters because some people have the most profound distortions. (One couple I saw wondered if pregnancy could be caused by French kissing. The wife had been taught as a teenager to put a magazine between her and the boy before sitting on his lap.)

Sexual problems are both a symptom and a cause of marital problems. Looking at sexual difficulties as a cause of marital distress, I focus rather early on sex because I know that if sex starts improving a lot of other conflicts diminish in importance. Pointless fighting and alienation take the place of sex. A number of the couples I see have not had sexual relations for some time; most of them think of sex as being the reward after years of therapy. I usually make a direct prescription that they start having sexual relations immediately—that night—and it usually works; it is as if a parent had given permission. (Incidentally, many couples report having sexual relationships the night of the therapy session; this frequency, which is greater than the increased frequency to be expected on weekends, is not an accident, I believe.) Reestablishing a sexual relationship, even if it consists of minimal physical contact by having couples sleep together again, often provides a base of motivation for the couple to work on their other problems. Thus, just as making other things better improves the sexual relationship, so making the sexual relationship better can help other areas improve. One prognostic factor as to whether a couple is going to make it in marital therapy is whether they are trying to regain something they once had with each other, or whether there was never much in their relationship to begin with. A close examination of the quality of the courtship and the early days of the marriage is required for this information. Generally speaking, when there was strong physical attraction in the past, sex has a greater chance of being rekindled than a marriage where sexual attraction was weak or tolerated in the beginning. As corny as it sounds, too, I often ask each partner the simple question, "Do you love your mate, using your own definition of love?" (One husband I asked this question of pulled out a slide rule and gave me a mathematical formula of his love for his wife.) This unscientific question often puts the therapy on a realistic basis and helps determine the direction the marriage is going to go.

Partners come to marital therapy with many different motives. Each person has a secret agenda which it is necessary to diagnose as soon as possible. Some partners come to marital therapy under false pretenses: The decision to divorce had been made privately and unilaterally beforehand and that person only goes through the motions of therapy. The husband may want to leave the wife in the hands of the therapist so he can leave guilt-free. As soon as I become aware of this strategy I expose it. Usually each person comes to marital therapy convinced that he or she is the wronged one and as soon as the mate's craziness, cruelty, or unreasonableness is revealed, the therapist will naturally concur. When this process operates in its extreme, with the other partner accepting all the blame, I switch things around and focus on the shortcomings of the blamer: Following the initial shock, the blamer is paradoxically relieved, and the whole complexion of the marriage relationship can be changed for the better with this technique.

One of the saddest situations seen in marital therapy is when one partner wants out of the marriage and the other desperately tries to hold on to the mate and grasps at any straw of hope that develops in the therapy. The person who is one-down and has no bargaining position does not dare go too far in honest leveling or complaining else the last tenuous tie be broken. The poignant suffering of these people is like those under a death sentence waiting for a reprieve. One can witness the pain in these people as their mates sever the ties of the relationship bit by bit (such as taking the ring off or confiding only in others). With each step away the heart breaks a bit more. The mate who is in the one-up position can exploit the one who cares more, yet also suffers from guilt. Some women feel pity for their rejected, begging husbands, for example, but they also feel contempt and are frightened by the husband's helplessness. It is particularly difficult for a male therapist to handle his feelings when he sees a man on his knees, crying and pleading for his wife not to leave him. Now *there is* an incident which can put a therapist's counter-transference feelings to the test!

Extra-marital affairs occur in the context of many of the situations I have mentioned. Like all sexual problems, affairs are only one aspect of the complexity of marital dynamics and are woven into the fabric of other problems. My clinical practice reveals a rather interesting trend, although my sample is small. Of the thirty-one couples I have seen where extra-marital affairs have occurred, in twenty-seven it was the woman who had the affair. There would seem to be some support for the observation that women are becoming more free sexually; also, one hears more complaints from wives that their husbands are not sexually responsive enough, whereas in previous years it used to be the other way around. So something seems to be happening. It is possible, however, that men are not as likely as women to regard an affair as something for which marital therapy is needed. What I mean by this is that a number of these women have telephoned for appointments, asking either to be seen alone for the first session so they can discuss whether their husband should know about the affair, or they set up the therapy sessions so as to tell the husband in a safe situation. Men seem less likely to handle it this way.

It is very difficult to make generalizations about affairs because they have idiosyncratic means in each situation, and the therapist must discern the particular significance and purpose of the affair for each case. Exploration can reveal that the affair was destructive in intent, designed to get rid of the mate; that it was a fortuitous by-product of other problems; that it had little to do with the mate at all; that it was consciously designed to arouse the mate's interest; that it was based on revenge for real or fancied wrongs; that the lover was a way-station on a route back to the mate (and in this sense the affair revived an empty marriage and was therapeutic), and so forth—the individual and transactional motives are infinite.

Let us now discuss this matter from the standpoint of the wife having had the affair because this is much more frequent statistically in my practice. A typical syndrome is that the couple have just been married a few years, and the woman feels neglected; she will say things like, "The romance is gone out of our marriage; I get my weekly ration of sex on Sunday night. Sex is mechanical and I feel like I am being used as a receptacle; he treats me like a piece of furniture" etc. The husband is usually a student or wrapped up in his work or sports on TV; he is usually quite reluctant to come to therapy—in some cases being dragged there. He does not feel they have any more problems than any other married couple, and he cannot understand what all the fuss is about. Many of these husbands are inarticulate. At this point the wife asks in a tentative way, "How would you feel if you found out I've had an affair?" Some people have such a need to use massive denial that they ignore the most obvious clues and hints and may even refuse to believe the overt disclosure of an affair with all of its details. The denial serves many functions: In some cases they do not want to hear it because then they would have to do something about it. Some husbands maintain a liberal, nonchalant attitude about the matter until the abstraction becomes a reality, until they know for sure. But I can feel the tension begin to rise in the room. The wife's toying with the idea of an affair as a possibility often leads the husband to ask finally, "What are you trying to tell me?" or, "We're not talking about what we're talking about, are we?" The range of reactions of the husbands when the abstract becomes real is very wide: At one extreme is the husband who said, "Great—right on, gal; I didn't think you had it in you;" to the other extreme where the man is truly devastated, deeply hurt, and rocked to the very foundations of his personality. Psychotic reactions, suicide, and murder in response to infidelity appear in the newspapers everyday, but when it is handled in conjoint marital therapy by a competent, well-trained marital or family therapist, and the meaning of the "infidelity" is explored, the dangers are minimized. There is no question that for some people this is the worst thing that can happen to them, and the most primitive passions of jealousy, revenge, depression, rage, and urges to murder are aroused: Some of these wives who set up the therapy to tell their husbands in that safe situation knew what they were about because they knew their husbands. (I might mention that these extreme reactions are a function of earlier, unconscious rejections being stirred up—but that is another story.) One can often detect in these people who react so extremely, a kind of mourning and grieving, tied in with the theme of lost love.

In the middle range of reactions, the husbands, on first hearing about the affair, usually react with mild upset and curiosity, and the impact does not hit them until the next day. Often the couple does not sleep that night, and the husband cannot go to work the next day. I can predict now when I will get a call for an extra session. The husband wants to start dealing with those crucial questions—Who with? How? When? Where? and the wife yells back, "Aren't you interested in *Why?*" It is important for the husband to know who the lover was, particularly whether it was someone he knew, perhaps his best friend. Some men press for all the explicit details, and others want to know nothing. Those who want to know everything are often fed all the details by the wives who sense it "turns on" their husbands. It is necessary to emphasize the multiple levels of the reactions in a given husband—on the one hand being excited and titillated at the image of the wife locked in a sexual embrace with another man, and on another level being horrified and sickened. The whore vs. pure virtuous woman dichotomy that all men have about women find its expression in intense sexual relations; The wives report that after the husbands found out about the affair they had the best sex they ever had, alternating with hurt, anger, accusations, and the kind of denial one has on hearing about the death of a loved one—"No! It *can't* be true!"

There are certain stages the couple go through around the affair. For varying periods of time the husband, needing to overcome what he perceives to be a castration, feels he is in competition with the lover and has to prove he is better. He will ask the wife, "Am I as good?" "I'll bet he never made you feel like that." "Hey, you didn't blow him, did you?" The couple get concerned about who knows about the affair, whether her family or his family or friends know. And the wife, who never experienced guilt about the affair at the time it was going on, is more likely to feel guilt now because someone besides herself knows about it. The projection of a superego is an interesting phenomenon; many people do not feel bad about what they have done until it becomes public knowledge. Another interesting aspect is that some of these husbands develop a close identification with the lover, who can become a fantasied superman who has stolen away his wife, or he can become a dissociated bad aspect of the self. Indeed, many of these men (and women, too, when they are in that position) seem to maintain an interest in the lover long after the one who has had the affair has lost interest. (One woman whose husband had told her of an affair followed her rival everywhere, saying, "That slut is everything I've struggled against all my life *not* to be.") Some of these people imagine during intercourse that they are the lover, and this brings about a kind of delicious torture. In most cases, the men are far more furious at the lover than at the wife, probably because it is safer; the feelings toward the wife are very mixed, because she is someone who is still needed, whereas the feelings toward the lover can be experienced as pure hatred. Still others are angry at their mates, partly because the confession has forced them to share in the guilt and responsibility. What is especially painful for these mates is the developing recognition that they did, in the majority of cases, play a part in the unfaithfulness of their mate.

Returning to the husbands who react with indifference or blandness to the announcement of the affair and do not even have a delayed response, the wife usually perceives this as the most hostile reaction of all, because it means they do not even care enough to get angry. One husband smiled through the whole thing until his wife hit him. Some husbands are over-forgiving and blame themselves, and still others have taken a scientific attitude about it, handling it like a research problem. Affairs are not all that difficult to end in the population I have been seeing. Usually there was not that much emotional involvement with the lover. One woman said she didn't miss the lover, but she missed the feeling of romance that the affair gave her.

Usually the women say that they would not marry their lovers; the husband may be looked upon as dull, but he is regarded as more substantial, responsible, and really caring. (One thing husbands hate to hear is, "I want to stay married to him for sensible reasons," or "because he's the father of my children.") The husband who has an affair may say he wants to stay married to his wife because she is a better homemaker and mother for his children than his girlfriend. Some men, in their efforts to woo back the wife, try to become more exciting to the wife, but it is very difficult to act glamorous when one feels depressed, has suppressed anger, and feels unable to compete with the lover. Feelings of rage, humiliation, and self-hatred about not being manly have to be balanced with the need to demonstrate to the wife a debonair, romantic image. This position is an untenable one to be in.

What are the consequences of affairs on the course of the therapy and the marriage? It is rare for the affair to break up the marriage in this special population. In most cases the couples move beyond this crisis and begin doing the real work of therapy. In some cases the affair helped create a whole new reinvigorated relationship for the couple. In others, the unfaithfulness gets incorporated into the sado-masochism, and the punishment continues for many years, always being dredged up in all future arguments. Sometimes I can stop the sado-masochism and tone down the feelings by suggesting a period of trial separation, utilizing Norman Paul's "split-freeze technique" of the partners separating and each spending time in individual exploration focused around the family of origin.

Some couples are unable to reestablish trust or a sense of the marital bond once unfaithfulness has occurred. Heightened suspiciousness can result in a process of checking up to see if the partner is where she is supposed to be; coming home a few minutes late can assume exaggerated importance. Sometimes the mate who has been errant is followed, or her husband may watch her eyes carefully at a party to see if they rest too long on another man. Often, connections are made, past events being reinterpreted in the light of the affair, and the "victim" may feel duped, saying, "What a fool I was to be so trusting." The event of unfaithfulness can also trigger previously hidden neurotic trends, and the affair can be used for private, neurotic purposes. For instance, a form of emotional blackmail may ensue whereby the person may demonstrate, in effect, "I can get away with anything; my faults count for nothing compared to what was done to me." Some continue to punish the partner, consciously in the form of being vindictive or flirting openly in front of the mate, and unconsciously by forgetting or by being impotent or frigid. There are those, too, who make a cause out of their partner's unfaithfulness, gaining the pity of friends and family.

There are many widely accepted professional beliefs which now and then are questioned. For instance, Murray Bowen has questioned the dictum that parents should always present a united front when disciplining children. More recently, on the question of divorce, some investigators question that the children are better off with one happy parent than two squabbling parents; they suggest that the kids may be more damaged by the sequelae of divorce than by living with unhappily married parents.

The dictum I am questioning at this time is whether honesty is always the best policy. At issue here—especially propagated by the encounter movement—is whether complete openness is always therapeutic. I am aware of the tremendous beneficial changes that can occur in the relationship when people level with each other, and for some marriages the disclosure of the affair was the best thing that could have happened. Some people, however, cannot cope with it, and I believe that some secrets should always remain secrets (e.g. one woman I saw had a son who was the child of another man, but neither her husband nor son knew this; this was a secret I respected.) Each situation has to be dealt with individually.

From the standpoint of individual psychology, sex is the arena for many motives other than sex—bolstering of self-esteem, testing of one's worth, being admired and desired, sex used as punishment or to degrade, as confirmation of one's identity, as a safe area in which to regress and be a child again, as fulfilling male passive wishes. (Have you ever noticed in pornographic films—which are made by men—the women are the aggressors and the men lay back and passively enjoy?) Those are some of the individual motives. Interactionally, when the mate does not respond as desired, motives are imputed to the partner—"If you do not lubricate, if you lose your erection, if you do not have an orgasm, or if you do not romance me before screwing, it means *you do not love me.*" This interpretation and assumption, which may or may not be true, then leads to the kinds of elaborate games that go on between couples—games that are often extremely difficult to unravel. (This has been beautifully illustrated in the film *Diary of a Mad Housewife.*) When a couple comes to a session in despair because sex was lousy all week, I have found it useful to examine in great detail the specific, concrete interactional events which led up to an unconsummated sexual act. Often when the wife is giving her messages that she is available, these are not picked up; on the other hand, it is difficult to make sure they were meant to be picked up. Sometimes the husband makes the sexual approach in a way calculated to get a refusal, or late at night after the TV programs are over, he may ask in a half-hearted way, trying to protect himself from an anticipated rejection. The husband may use his wife's problems (e.g. her frigidity) as protection against his own anxieties about sex; some of these men get panicky if the wife is unreservedly receptive. Occasionally, a mate will pick a fight during the day in order to make sure that sex will not take place that night. A series of prior conditions may be set up: "If you'll buy me that dress; if you'll get it over with as soon as possible; if you'll listen first to how you made me angry that day." Women use stalling tactics such as: their period is not over; wearing a nightgown the husband hates; giggling or crying during the act itself. Husbands may say they are tired or they have been drinking and fall asleep; or they do not want to "bother" their wives too much. Usually, the basic problem is mutual fear of intimacy.

One question which keeps coming up in marital therapy is whether monogamy can work, and if so, how? This question has troubled people for thousands of years, and its urgency rises and falls according to the changing cultural norms. It is an acute question in our society. There are many partners today who close their eyes to the affairs of their mates; some can tolerate their partners having physical sex but are very threatened by an emotional relationship between the mate and someone else. Some handle the problem by having homosexual relationships (which seem to be increasing) and others by participating in swingers groups. (One couple thought they would like to answer their marital problem by each having discreet affairs without it affecting their marriage, and they asked my professional opinion as to whether that was likely to work. I expressed my doubts, based on my experience, and the statement was made, "But doc, if it was working out well, you wouldn't know it would you?" And he is right—they would not come to therapy.) There is a great deal of turmoil and confusion about faithfulness in these times, and we certainly do not have many answers. One of the interesting things about the new publication *Sexual Behavior* is how the experts differ on questions like these!

Let me now mention briefly some of the therapy methods I have used in dealing with marital problems. I believe that the most powerful treatment method in existence is family therapy, and as often as I can, I try to have sessions with these married adults and their families of origin. This is where it is *really* at (as in the film, *I Never Sang for My Father*)—which is one of the reasons, I suppose, why most people become very anxious when the suggestion is first broached. I have seen husbands and wives go into panic at the thought of bringing in their parents and brothers and sisters: They are afraid that their parents will go crazy, die of a heart attack, or that the therapist will kill them in some way. Once they can see the purpose, they even become eager to bring them in (not to tell off the parents, but to open up honest communication and take positions for themselves: then I also help other family members as well), and like a pebble thrown into a stream, all kinds of ripples and repercussions develop: Both the patient and I get calls asking us, "What in hell are you trying to do—ruin our family?" Those who can persist and do undergo these sessions usually find them rewarding; the greatest therapeutic changes in individuals I have seen have occurred with this method—which in turn improves the marriage relationship. It is the best way to find out who you really are.

The most frequent initial complaint I hear from couples is "lack of communication"—trite, but the phrase is true. Many married people simply do not deal with the issues between them; they communicate by behavior—sulking, giving disguised hints, having affairs, bickering and nagging—and the mate is expected to be a mind-reader and decode the messages. The appropriate kind of leveling, as painful as it may be, is one of the first therapeutic steps one has to take. In this connection, I have found some of George Bach's ideas on constructive fighting very useful.

Another therapy method I have been using with good results is couples group therapy. Initially, I used the method as a way of handling my own feelings: Some couples were boring, some aroused anger, some were too intent on using me as a judge, some hit a plateau and could not move; some could not stop fighting; I put them in groups in order to free myself from the transference-counter-transference jam. In the group situations, the transference gets diluted, and I can use the group process for therapeutic leverage. As usually happens in a situation like this, I discovered that couples group therapy is a powerful form of treatment in its own right. In this permissive atmosphere, the couples compare their problems with those in other marriages (e.g. sexually liberated and prudish couples can help each other); they use other marriages as models of how something can be worked out or what to avoid. It is not uncommon for a couple leaving the first session to say, "My God, I thought our marriage was bad!" Better reality testing can be done in the group so that the couples can be confronted with their inferences and assumptions about each other. Co-therapists are particularly helpful in couples group therapy.

Finally, I want to mention a few words about "divorce therapy." Most people laugh when they hear that expression and say, "Aren't you trying to save marriages?" I have found some situations where divorce is advisable between people who are truly allergic to each other; in most of these cases the decision to divorce occurred before they started therapy. My task is to help the partners disengage from their relationship with dignity and with the least amount of self- or other-destructiveness so they can be free to form new relationships. Most people find divorce a heart-breaking, painful process; when there has been intense emotional investment in each other, the partners can only separate savagely. The vituperation and acrimony surrounding divorce proceedings can become most bitter, and few can resist using the children as weapons. Incidentally, with these couples I try to assist not only with the disengagement process, but have them work out arrangements on practical matters, such as division of property, visitation rights, support, etc., because in a therapeutic atmosphere some reason can prevail, whereas the minute lawyers come into the picture it is a whole new ballgame and often gets out of hand. (We still have too many unrealistic divorce laws where legally there has to be a guilty or injured party.) Most people who get divorced maintain contact, and many people continue with the bitterness toward the ex-mate for a lifetime. Divorce therapy can help prevent that, and by including the children in some sessions, we can help them come to terms with the divorce in a way that their own future lives and marriages will not be seriously affected.

I do not want to end on the subject of divorce, even though it can be looked upon as an opportunity. Life's greatest challenge is the ability to make the exceedingly complex adjustment to another person in marriage, to tolerate in each other the working through of ambivalent internal objects, to permit each other's regression, all of which infantile strivings are embedded in the context of bonds of affection, commitment, the process of give and get, the acceptance of adult responsibility, and the overflow of love to the children.

DEPTH AND PARADOX IN MARITAL RELATIONSHIPS

Commentary: Ivan Boszormenyi-Nagy

The issue of marital therapy is an excellent one for focusing on the difference between the family therapy or familial dynamic points of view and the individual dynamic or marriage counselling point of view. Although as Dr. Framo has indicated, the language of relational dynamics has not even been sufficiently developed, nonetheless, it is the obligation of the family therapist to spell out the fundamental difference of his premises from that of the other approaches. Aside from these new premises, the family approach as such offers itself as the source of an integrative, comprehensive framework. Yet, the ideally projected comprehensive and dynamic clinical framework of the future should include also the contributions and conceptual tools of individual psychodynamic theory.

Marital therapy issues, like other family relational matters, are usually discussed in power dynamic terms. The comparative positional strength of the sexes and the intensity of the self-serving needs of each individual spouse could be seen as leading to a continuous power conflict and competitive struggle as the ongoing context of the relationship. The significance of power conflicts notwithstanding, family relational forces are more deeply grounded in the basic existential dimensions of the commitment, mutual enhancement and exploitation between persons, and in fundamental loyalty to one's family of origin. In effect, marriage conflicts very often reflect the underlying overt or covert loyalty conflicts between the two families of origin, each represented by one spouse.

The question of sexual satisfaction and fidelity obtains a new viewpoint from the perspective of deep relational dynamics. The question of mutual sexual satisfaction in a marriage depends on much deeper dynamic factors than are ordinarily considered.

Whereas it is true that the individual's psychological development, especially regarding his super-ego and guilt configurations, is significant, an important component is guilt over disloyalty to one's family of origin as a determinant of guilt about sex. Although Freud's original constructs of Oedipal conflict are coined in the psychological context of pleasure versus guilt, it is easy to see a disloyalty aspect in the Oedipal situation, especially as it implies insult to the parent of the same sex. However, it is the common observation of family therapists that in many families the adolescent and young adult member faces great amounts of guilt over disloyalty to both parents by simply depriving themselves in individuation and separation process. The parents validate their child's guilt by the usually unintended display of their unhappiness over being abandoned. Later on, the marriage of the child can in itself symbolize filial disloyalty. Viewed in this context, it is interesting to see that in many marriages, having an affair or even dissolving the marriage and entering into a second marriage is experienced not so much as marital disloyalty but rather as implicit filial loyalty. As the original marriage meant disloyalty to the family of origin, the new relationship means restitution through betrayal of that which itself has been treacherous. Perhaps at the expense of sacrificing the first marriage one can expiate one's guilt to one's family of origin.

An important aspect of sexual guilt is based on the social dimension of distributive justice. By this it is meant that any member of a social group who receives more gratification or has more fortunate circumstances than the others becomes somewhat resented, envied, and censured by the majority of that group. Without having done harm to anyone, a more fortunate member of any community will begin to feel guilty over his relative excess of gratification and over the relative disappointment of the others. This aspect of social dynamics can easily add to the already existing guilt over disloyalty to one's parents when it comes to sexual freedom or pleasure in marriages. The sex therapist, the family therapist, or even the individual psycho-therapist, by endorsing the goal of increased gratification in the family member or spouse, will automatically side with that part of distributive justice that gives social approval to the patient's increased gratification.

By certain mechanisms of loyalty even ambivalent resentment of one's parents can serve as a basis of renouncing one's marriage. On one hand, *by the laws of retributive justice*, one is impelled, to repay one's frustration, disappointment or hurt feelings, even to the parent; on the other hand, one's obligation to his parents makes it difficult and ethically wrong to hurt those parents. As a result, in an unconscious defense of one's filial loyalty, one can mete out the retributive punishment to one's spouse and thereby spare the parents. Such an action though unfair and inappropriate, will not result in guilt feelings because of one's relief over the lowered level of guilt of disloyalty to his family of origin. Such punishment or scapegoating of the marital relationship can take indirect and covert forms also. For instance, much that appears to be fear of intimacy can actually be based on guilt over disloyalty to one's family of origin. This is often seen in couples who, paradoxically, lose their capacity for sexual togetherness shortly after they formalize their loyalty commitment to each other. Naturally, they also have formalized their relative disloyalty of their family of origin through marriage at the same time.

A related question is whether or not monogamy can work. Whereas it is usually discussed in terms of its restrictions on sexual freedom, monogamy can also be vulnerable to guilt of disloyalty to one's family or origin because of its requirements of primary loyalty commitment to a new nuclear family. This is especially applicable to the young nuclear family of today's Western World. Whereas in old times or in traditional parts of the world the extended family or large clan surrounded the new couple, in the contemporary West frequently it is as if all or most of the new couple's ties with the family of origin were being cut off. This seeming over-commitment to monogamy and the nuclear family makes them vulnerable to conflicts based on invisible loyalty.

One more preponderance of vertical versus horizontal commitments in relationships is that family therapists are not likely to regard marriages mainly from the point of view of the two contracting spouses. One main reason for this difference between family therapy and marriage counselling lies in the important considerations of each spouse's necessary overt or covert loyalty to his or her family of origin. Another important vertical dimension is the couple's obligation and loyalty to their children or prospective children. The interests of the children are important determinants of that which becomes a covert, possibly undischarged obligation and therefore a source of guilt in both spouses. Therefore, family therapists cannot consider marital therapy or even divorce therapy in isolation from its impact on the interests of the children.

The foregoing conclusions have broader implications for society than as mere guidelines for psychotherapy. The understanding of the deeper relational structure of marriages and nuclear families has great importance in judicial decisions about divorces, child custody, visitation rights of parents, adoption, foster arrangements and design for the care of the aged. Without an integrated view of multigenerational, vertical existential commitments, only the more superficial aspects of close relationships can be understood.

A WAY OF LOOKING

Commentary: Virginia Satir

I am so used to looking at things a certain way that perhaps I am already contaminated by what I am thinking. One of the points I am trying to make is that if we look with *new* eyes, what we look at becomes clearer. What we are seeing may be something that was there that we had not seen before. This is something I would like to leave open for myself, because I am turning around as though I suddenly do not know anything, and this is extremely hard to do. But I think it is important now to view things this way.

There is something else that I relate to, and it has to do with making choices. In the family sculpturing presented earlier, we could talk about any subject—desks, sex, money—and it would all have more or less the same outcome. A therapist could not really use it well because of the way in which it was communicated and contaminated. And I am reminded of a young group of adolescents I was treating at one point, all of whom had "sexual acting-out." This merely meant that they had their penises and vaginas in the wrong places at the wrong time, and they scared people about it. What I did with them was to help them get in touch with their affective selves. We did all kinds of things that had to do with workings of the body. (It is phenomenal, to me, how few people are in touch with their feelings; they think they are feeling but they do not *feel* their feeling.) We did not say anything about sex. What we did was to come in touch with the wholeness of the person through this affective thing. So, in a funny kind of way, the talk about sex may not be where it really is. What it may really be is our own *wholeness* and being in touch with this whole being we have, or seeing or thinking or feeling and so on, and being willing to do that. So trying to know which is the leaf and which is the twig and which is the trunk and which are the roots, for me, means that one is not more important than the other. It is important, however, to know what we are talking about so that when we have to relate it, we can do it in a more meaningful fashion.

Commentary: Geraldine Spark

Only a small percentage of people experiment with new forms of marriage: the bigamous marriage, communal, corporate, open-ended, linear, and other arrangements. Since there is an eternal human need for reliability, security, long-time commitment, care, and concern, marriage is here to stay. Disappointments and failures will continue if hope is placed in these external changes in marriage, as if the new arrangements were improved alternatives to traditional marriage. A myth that needs to be dispelled is that mere openness or directness will automatically create improvements. Similarly, just teaching young people sexual techniques will not touch the core problems.

What is needed is some kind of pre- and post-marital preparation to help people recognize a *capacity for compromise.* How many young people believe that it will take hard work and continual adjustments on their part as they move through the ever-changing phases of marriage and family life? Although it is generally accepted that children go through phases and parents must change accordingly, the marital relationship is rarely conceived as a demanding and changing relationship. Balancing the emotional and sexual intimacy of the peer marital relationship requires as much or more time and effort than the parental one.

Sexual difficulties within the marital relationship are often symptomatic of difficulties in other areas of the marriage: money, health, children, jobs, grandparents, and in-laws. Sexual functioning is connected with my feelings about myself as an individual, as a wife, and mother. It is equally interlocked with my parents' marriage and family life. My sexuality is not a result of what my mother told me about menstruation and sexual relations. It developed from my experiences with my parents and from observing their marital relationship: How my parents negotiated their differences; who gave what, and when; when and how compassion and tenderness were expressed; how anger, hostility, and despair were dealt with. The direct sexual inter-locking can be seen in the following illustration:

> A young married woman and her middle-aged mother were in daily phone or visiting contact; one would not purchase a dress without the other. They both came to a session. The young woman turned to her mother and with tears said, "Mother, why am I frigid? You never talked to me about sex—why not?"
>
> Her mother also started to cry as she said, "After forty years of marriage, I have never experienced any pleasure. I told you it is a wife's duty to accommodate her husband."

This was not only an exceptional sharing of personal experiences, but it helped remove the mother from being the blamed person, being also a sexually deprived woman.

In our clinical population, there is frequently minimal or no sexual relations between the marital pair. It still surprises me that the couples in our families—in their thirties and forties—have so little sex. This is despite the pill, abortion availability, and open talk about sex in the communications media. In my parents' generation the subject was almost taboo; contraception was not perfected, and the role of woman/mother was almost stereotyped. How are sexual feelings channeled in the families we see? The clinician may hear more about it from the children than the adults: who is sleeping with whom; who does or does not belong together; the lack of bathroom and bedroom privacy. If the therapist brings up the issues of excessive stimulation and seduction of children, he may be told, "You have a dirty mind." A father sleeps through the night in the bed of his twelve-year-old daughter and cannot understand why she had night-mares! A child is glued to the wall adjoining his parents' bedroom and reports to the siblings on the marital fights which occur because of sexual incompatibility.

The marital relationship and sexuality in a family has other generational dimensions connected with unfinished dependency needs, loyalty implications of indebtedness, and filial responsi-bility to one's aging parents. The capacity to function at a sexually and emotionally mature level not only depends upon resolution of intrapsychic conflicts, but also on rebalancing of loyalty commitments and obligations in a three-generational family context.

Question: How are children used by the spouses in the process of separation and divorce (*implications for treatment*)?

Answer: I prefer not to limit my answer only to divorce. Children may also be blamed or exploited by adults for money troubles, sexual difficulties, lack of social and family contacts. In many instances, there are valid reasons in the marriage for two people separating and divorcing. But for some, the unfinished business with the family of origin is projected onto or lived out with the mate or children. Too frequently, feelings of inadequacy, failure, and despair are taken out on others because of a need for revenge, retaliation, etc. Many persons are used and hurt as a result of repetitious situations—children, adults, grandparents, and in some instances even a future mate. These children and adults are caught in an untenable loyalty bind—taking sides one against another as a way of protecting themselves and each other.

5

A Family Therapist Looks at The Problem of Incest*

G. PIROOZ SHOLEVAR

THE JUDICIARY AND most psychotherapists handle the problem of incest between father and daughter as a problem arising primarily from the weakness of the father, conventionally considered to be an ego and super-ego defect. Traditionally, no family evaluation was included in order to rule out disorders of the family system which could lead to incestuous behavior. Based on this belief, the courts put the fathers in prison or on probation, in some cases without psychiatric or psychological evaluation, and often without psychiatric treatment.

The view of fathers as the only disturbed member of the family could go a long way in support of familial distortions. For example, it helps other family members deny their contributions to the problem. It is clear that this view results in a disposition which does not take cognizance of family interactions and dynamics and too often leads to an unnecessary family break-up.

Family therapy as a treatment modality was not included in reviews of treatment of sexual offenses in the 1960's. Considering that the sexual relationship is an important function of marriage, one would logically expect a look at marriage in cases of manifest sexual disorders.

A few general points need to be stated in order to clarify the theoretical position of the family therapist. Family therapy does not consider the behavior of a person as arising primarily

* Reprinted with permission from *The Bulletin of The American Academy of Law and Psychiatry.* Volume 3, No. 1, 1975.

from sources within the individual. It contends that forces within the family motivate adaptive and unadaptive behavior on the part of the family member. Developments in the past two decades indicate a family member may develop a behavioral symptom in order to elicit a supportive response from his spouse and thereby change their relationship in a direction more desirable to him. The symptom in a family member can also be a product of how he is being involved or used in the conflict of other family members (Ackerman, 1958; Haley, 1963; Sholevar, 1970). In the latter sense, a child may develop a symptom as a result of conflict between his parents.

These theoretical views carry certain implications for technique. The patterns of interaction within the family are often poorly understood or frequently unrecognized by individual family members. Therefore, to rely exclusively on verbal reports by family members of family interaction is to be too easily misled and deprived of essential data in the treatment process (Ackerman, 1958; Nagy, 1965). Accordingly, it is necessary to work with the whole family to observe interaction and personal transactions in order to evaluate the strengths and conflicts within the family as they unfold in the treatment process.

An illustration of dynamics in a family with sexually offensive behavior is given by the late Dr. Nathan Ackerman in his book *Treating the Troubled Family* (Ackerman, 1966).* It is a verbatim account of an interview with a young couple after the husband had been arrested for exhibiting himself in public. The wife had responded to the incident with indignation, a feeling of shock and a wish to desert her husband.

In the family treatment, it was learned that the couple had not been able to have sexual intercourse during their six years of marriage. The couple had many fears, immaturities, and inhibitions regarding sex. The wife's fear of intercourse and pregnancy had resulted in her making it impossible for her husband to penetrate her. The husband then sought reassurance

---

* Incest has been recognized as a "family affair" and described in literature by J. W. Mohr et al., M. Lewis et al., I. Kaufman et al., R. E. L. Masters (ed.), J. W. Rinehart, I. B. Weiner and D. Langsley et al. in the 60's.

for his masculinity by exposing himself publicly. Here the internal and interpersonal conflicts of the couple had remained unresolved and had resulted in conflict between the family and the social community.

In the interview, Dr. Ackerman dealt with all levels of sexual conflict within the family, from their internal conflicts about their sexual roles, to marital and interpersonal conflicts which had resulted in an unconsummated marriage. He helped the couple to deal with their conflict on the intrafamilial level rather than to displace it outward to the level between the family and society through the husband's action. A few weeks following this family session, the couple succeeded in having their first sexual intercourse after six years of marriage.

This is an instructive example of how the defensive maneuvers of the family, in attempting to contain a conflict, bring the family into conflict with society. It also illustrates how easily the wife declares herself innocent and her husband guilty and expresses the wish to leave him. The latter point is also a significant finding and we will return to it later.

Data and Scope

It is the goal of this report to make observations for a possible relationship between overall family interactions and the incestuous involvement of family members. The report presents data on three lower-middle-class black families who were brought into court when the fathers were convicted of sexual involvement with their daughters or stepdaughters. All three involvements had resulted in the daughters becoming pregnant. The fathers were enrolled in individual or group psychotherapy on order of the court, but there were joint interviews with the men and their wives because of the interest of the author.

Case 1: The J. Family consisted of Mr. and Mrs. J. and three children. Mrs. J. was raised on a farm by strict parents who did not send her to school and did not give her any sexual information or education. The parents accompanied her and her sister to the "outhouse" even when they were grown up, so that boys did not have a chance to approach them. Mrs. J.'s parents were an unhappy couple, and her mother constantly harped on her father. Mrs. J. did not know about the relationship between menstrual periods, sexual intercourse, and pregnancy until she became pregnant out of wedlock. She gave birth to her oldest daughter, Gail, at the age of seventeen. Mrs. J. married when Gail was three years old. Mrs. J. was very unhappy, resented the sexual relationship, and was cold and rejecting toward her husband's sexual advances, particularly after their frequent fights.

Mrs. J. "discovered" the sexual involvement of her husband and Gail when the daughter became pregnant by Mr. J. at the age of thirteen. Mrs. J. was working and was pregnant herself with her second child at this time. Gail was sent to her grandmother, and the grandmother arranged for an abortion. The incest was not brought to the attention of a psychiatric clinic or court, and the family reunited following Gail's abortion. Gail kept walking around the house nude, and the mother continued her denial of Mr. J.'s attraction to her daughter. In all likelihood, there were continued incidents of sexual intercourse between Gail and her stepfather during the three years following her abortion. At the end of this period, the mother found Gail and Mr. J. in bed together. She put her daughter in the Youth Study Center and brought charges against her husband. At this time, Mrs. J. was pregnant for the third time. A few months later, the couple separated, and the mother brought Gail home.

Five years later, Mrs. J. contacted a child psychiatric clinic, wishing to put her twelve-year-old son away because of his destructive behavior and fecal soiling. (She also thought her son's penis was deformed; it was actually a slight adhesion.) She thought her ex-husband had put "roots" (curse) on her. She was angry, depressed, socially isolated, had no contact with men, and disliked them. At times, she felt she had done her husband wrong and wished she had kept her husband and had put her daughter away. Her oldest daughter, Gail, was just married and was running around with other men (while mother was babysitting for her). The youngest daughter (aged four) was doing well.

In spite of the improvement of his fecal soiling, constipation, and aggressive behavior, Mrs. J. insisted on institutionalizing her son for the protection of the boy. The mother did not want to have her son at home on weekends, and the infrequent home visits were joyless, and the mother and son remained distant. Their relationship was only partially modified after two years of institutionalization.

CASE 2:   The K. Family consisted of Mr. and Mrs. K., who were in their thirties and had a 15-year-old daughter. Their marriage was characterized by the couple's complete inability to compromise or settle their differences. Their many fights were followed by Mrs. K. rejecting the repeated sexual demands of her husband when in bed. The wife found an easy solution for this problem by putting her daughter in bed between herself and her husband, since the daughter was seven or eight-years-old. This stopped her husband from forceful demands while the wife refused him sexually, and it undoubtedly exposed the daughter to much sexual stimulation at the same time.

When the daughter was twelve-years-old, Mr. K. had to make several trips to another state to visit his dying father and later to participate in his funeral. The trips drained the family savings and put them into debt. The financial problems further deteriorated the marital relationship, particularly when Mrs. K. was forced to take a job. She then absolutely refused to have sexual intercourse with her husband. She stayed out at night or returned home very late. Mr. K. started running around with other women and drinking but still missed his wife. It was during this period that Mr. K. became sexually involved with his twelve-year-old daughter while his wife was staying out. The daughter became pregnant, and the wife brought charges against her husband. She wanted to leave him but eventually decided to stay. The daughter had an abortion. Mr. K. was put on probation with mandatory psychiatric treatment. Mrs. K. did not undergo any psychiatric treatment.

CASE 3:   The P. Family consisted of Mr. and Mrs. P., who were in their mid-thirties, and a sixteen-year-old daughter. Mr. P. was a steady worker and Mrs. P. was a fanatically religious woman. The marital dissatisfaction was readily apparent. Mr. P.

in an urgent manner demanded much affection from his wife who gave all her time and attention to the church. The rejecting attitude of Mrs. P. was most apparent when her husband made sexual demands which she discarded as dirty and inappropriate. Her sexual refusal was difficult for her husband who had such a strong sexual drive that he once had to stop his car on the shoulder of a highway to achieve sexual relief by masturbation. Later, the husband became interested in cunnilingus intercourse, but it was met with absolute refusal on his wife's part. The sexual rejection by Mrs. P. and her frequent absences from the home resulted in sexual involvement of the angry and dissatisfied father with their daughter, who at the time was thirteen-years-old. She became pregnant and the father was put on probation with mandatory psychiatric treatment. The daughter's pregnancy was terminated by abortion.

The couple's sexual difficulty continued, much to the distress and frustration of Mr. P. Since the husband was the labeled offender and criminal, the wife felt justified in refusing to participate in marital therapy. She continued to be absent from home frequently and for a few days at a time, knowing well her husband's strong sexual desires and the possibility of repetition of what had happened in the past. At these times, Mr. P. required frequent support from a psychiatrist in order to prevent himself from involvement with his daughter.

When the daughter was fourteen and one-half-years-old, she became pregnant by a man who was doing some work in their home. This was not discovered until the girl was six months pregnant. Mr. P. was furious and wanted to shoot the man; Mrs. P. just wanted her daughter out of the house. Much support was needed to prevent Mrs. P. from rejecting her daughter completely, and the daughter was placed in a hospital for unwed mothers. The marriage continued with sexual dissatisfaction and the wife's absorption in church activities. The mandatory treatment was finished when Mr. P. and his daughter resumed the sexual relationship, resulting in the daughter's third pregnancy at the age of fifteen. Mr. P. was imprisoned, and Mrs. P. continued with her volunteer church activities.

Discussion

A final look at these families casts some doubt on the conventional view of the incestuous family. Such a view indicates that the father is a sexually dangerous and aggressive animal who seduces his innocent daughter in many cleverly hideous ways which cannot be detected by highly advanced devices of a solicitous mother whose only goal is the protection of her daughter against sexual molestation. A more likely picture indicates a couple with long-standing difficulties in attaining sexual adjustment and satisfaction. The husbands were men who became overwhelmed by a grown woman who resisted them in an unreasonable manner. Left with their strong sexual urges, they could not find appropriate outlets for these urges. The wives were sexually cold toward their husbands or had a general contempt for men. The solicitiousness and protectiveness of the mothers for their daughters are questionable. The mothers had gone out of their way to leave their husbands and daughters alone, being well aware of the possibility of repetition of past events. They were also aware of the sexual dissatisfaction of the fathers and of their anger. The fact that incestuous relationships were reported only after the daughters' pregnancies raises a question about the mothers' genuine interest in the welfare of their children. The pregnancies were also discovered too late for abortion in two instances. One would expect an interested mother to discover the pregnancies earlier.

In the P. Family, the mother had taken no protective measure against her daughter's involvement with a man outside the family. In a similar case of incest brought to the attention of the court, the wife was to leave home to visit a relative. The husband threatened to get the daughter intoxicated with wine and have sexual relations with her if the wife left home. When the wife left, he gave the daughter some wine, took her to the bedroom and removed her panties. The girl's resistance and screaming brought some people upstairs to her rescue before completion of the sexual act. (There had probably been prior incestuous involvement in this family.)

The mothers seem much more committed to pursuing their

own desires and wishes rather than protecting their daughters or satisfying their husbands' needs. This is clear in the P. family when Mrs. P. spends much of her time establishing new churches, thereby leaving her daughter and her husband alone. Here again the mother covertly encourages the incestuous act. Mrs. K. was also more concerned with avoiding the sexual advances of her husband toward herself rather than protecting her daughter who slept in the same bed with her father in an empty house. These examples also illustrate the great sensitivity of the men in incestuous families to abandonment by their wives.

A long-standing, unsatisfactory marital relationship was the rule. Although the dissatisfaction was more pronounced in the sexual area, it was present in all aspects of the marital relationships. The differences and disagreements were never settled to the point of solution and satisfaction. Following disagreements each partner went his own way without consulting the other. The following examples illustrate the degree of unrelatedness of such couples.

The E. Family were in their twenties. The wife did not enjoy the sexual relationship, and the husband felt guilty for her lack of sexual enjoyment. The wife did not want to become pregnant, but they could not decide on a contraceptive device and practiced withdrawal before ejaculation. The husband intentionally made her pregnant by not withdrawing, which infuriated her. After the child was born, she refused to take care of the baby and remained negative toward their child.

The wife in a Catholic family rejected her husband's frequent sexual advances because of fear of pregnancy, while refusing to use contraceptive devices which were against her belief. The opinion and the wish of the husband did not matter, and there was eventual involvement with their young daughter. Episodes such as running high bills on a secret charge account rather than planning the income of the family were also present.

The role of the daughters or stepdaughters in incestuous families is poorly understood. The possibility of active involvement of the victim in an incestuous act needs to be studied. The failure of the daughters to reveal the involvement may not be related to fear of punishment by the father, but to other factors, such as their own pleasure or the belief that the mothers would not listen to them. Most of the daughters had great empathy for their fathers. They felt their mothers were depriving the fathers, and they had to compensate for what the fathers were not receiving; they felt that by sexual compensation, the fathers' social functioning would be restored.

Apparently, the daughters develop exaggerated seductiveness and precocious sexuality which fits in and serves a function in the defective marital relationships of their parents. Some of these daughters show a strong tendency to repeat the same action and relationship in future situations. In the P. Family, the daughter became involved with and pregnant by a married man in the neighborhood who did some work in their home. In another family, the teenage daughter and her father were involved in frequent and regular sexual relationships, but the "mother did not want to hear about it." Eventually, the conflicts heightened, and the girl was thrown out of the house. The nextdoor neighbors felt sorry and took her in, but in a few days it was discovered that the neighbor's husband and the daughter had become involved sexually and she had to leave the neighbor's house.

The use of the daughter in the family conflict results in an age-inappropriate and unadaptive behavior, with some daughters claiming the rights of a grown woman, particularly their exclusive rights to have and keep their babies.

In the group therapy experience of the author, it is not an uncommon phenomenon to observe a young woman who usually has many difficulties with her husband shock the group by revealing her protracted sexual relationships with her father in her childhood. She then proceeds to dominate the group by repeatedly diverting the group from all other topics to speak of these incidents in a seductive and shocking manner. Usually, these women had revealed their early experiences to their husbands in the beginning of the marriage and later use it in order to keep themselves in a special position. For example, one demanded that her husband leave her alone sexually because she could not enjoy sex due to her early experience, whereas she was very seductive with other men.

The substitution of daughter for mother as a sexual object seems to be a function of poor differentiation in incestuous families. In this way, they are similar to what Murray Bowen describes as "undifferentiated ego mass families." Lack of role clarity, function, and position make these families particularly susceptible to such substitution. A low level of functioning, particularly the inability to deal with strong feelings without relative weakening of reality testing in a specific area, goes along with poor differentiation. As Bowen (1966) points out, the feelings run high in poorly differentiated families due to lack of necessary structures. This clouds the boundaries in the family picture. When the incestuous families are faced with mounting sexual desires and heightened anger following departure of the mother, the undifferentiation increases and the daughter appears sufficiently similar to the mother to substitute her as a sexual object.

It is doubtful if many incestuous families make an attempt to consult an outside agency, such as clergy, marriage counselor, or mental health facility, in order to change their conflictual patterns of living. They seem particularly reluctant to bring an outsider in on their problems. Clinically, there seem to be two extreme groups in dysfunctional and symptomatic families. The extreme group on one side attempts to cure all their ills by bringing in outsiders. The views of members in the family have little significance, and such families can be involved with many agencies, neighbors, clergy, etc. The group on the opposite extreme attempts to cure their ills by expulsion of a family member. The latter usually blame one of the members as the exclusive source of conflict in a scapegoating manner and seek relief by expulsion of such a member. The expulsion can be in the form of institutionalization in a therapeutic or correctional facility or family estrangement through banishment. It appears as though "expulsive families" strive toward a more normal balance by limiting the size of their membership and extruding the member they view as the weakest link in the chain of membership. Such families can be very resistant to the entry of an agent of change such as a therapist. It is highly possible that incestuous families belong to the "expulsive group" of families. For example, banishment and estrangement of the family in the J. family was later followed by institutionalization of the son. Mrs. J. insisted on putting her son away and did so in spite of the symptomatic improvement of his constipation, soiling, and aggressive behavior. These families do not voluntarily ask for assistance from outside and only participate in treatment under pressure from the court. For example, Mrs. P. did not discuss any of her problems with her minister despite the protracted time they spent together. If it is indeed a characteristic of these families to deal with family conflicts by expelling a family member, the action of the court to send the father to prison will perpetuate the family conflicts rather than promote a healthy alliance of the members. Even in the case of immediate relief, it can result in transfer of symptoms to another family member such as the development of soiling and aggressive behavior in the son in the J. Family. Expulsion of the father also did not prevent the involvement of the daughter with another man in the P. Family.

Conclusion

Like other symptoms, incestuous behavior can develop when the coping mechanisms of the family can no longer manage family conflicts without violating the continuity of the system. Thus, in one sense, the incestuous behavior is an expression of the family's effort to solve its problems and create a new state of equilibrium with a more manageable level of dissonance. But like all primarily defensive behavior, it rarely achieves an enduring pattern of wholesome social balance in the family. This is because the family continues with its defective relationships and erratic communication, further burdened by the consequences of incestuous behavior.

This report does not intend to make generalizations about the dynamics of incestuous families. Such formulations can be proposed only after systematic and controlled studies of a variety of such families have been made in conjoint sessions to observe the subtle interactional processes between family members. This chapter has limited itself to presenting data from a few lower-middle class families with overt incestuous involvement between the family members.

The three cases described above and a majority of cases of incest were brought to the attention of the community only after the daughters had become pregnant. This raises the point that many incestuous relationships go unreported due to the absence of pregnancies which will force them into the open. What is questioned is the working assumption of the judiciary and many psychotherapists that the incestuous act is the result of short-comings in the personality structure of the father. We believe that more attention should be paid to the overall relationships between family members in order to understand the multiple forces resulting in incestuous behavior.

It is therefore recommended that courts and mental health centers request assessment of the whole family in conjoint family sessions in place of or in addition to individual assessment of the father. This will provide a broader picture of the situation and can prevent inadvertent siding with the destructive and unhealthy forces within the family. The courts should also be alert to their important roles and duty in dealing with the problem of incest. If it is a property of such families to resist involvement in treatment, it is the court alone which is in a position to request mandatory family assessment and treatment.

REFERENCES

Ackerman, Nathan W.: *Psychodynamics of Family Life.* New York, Basic Books, 1958.
Ackerman, Nathan: *Treating Troubled Families.* New York, Basic Books, 1966.
Bowen, Murray: The use of family theory in clinical practice. *Compr Psychiatry,* 345-374, 1966.
Bowen, Murray: Personal communication.
Haley, Jay: *Strategies of Psychotherapy.* New York, Grune and Stratton, 1964.
Haley, Jay: The families of the schizophrenic: A model system. *J Nerv Ment Dis, 129:*357-374, 1959.
Boszormenyi-Nagy, I., and Framo, J. L.: *Intensive Family Therapy.* New York, Hoeber Medical Div., Har-Row, 1965.
Sholevar, G. Pirooz: Family therapy. *J of Albert Einstein Med Center,* Philadelphia, *18:* No. 2, 1970.

Commentary: Richard Crocco

How a therapist defines a family problem clinically and in his own family determines how he practices family psychotherapy. One wonders how often a professional is hindered by the concept of incest in attempting to develop close personal relationships with each parent. Because of the great deal of personal energy I put into phone contacts, letters, and person-to-person relationships with my mother, it might be misconstrued as something incestuous! Cut-offs from parents are usually best understood as flowing from a three-generational family transmission process than from individual constructs of unconscious fears of incest, etc.

Scheflen and Ferber discuss the unfortunate myth, officially sanctioned by mental health and welfare professionals, that the isolated nuclear family is a biologically necessary structure as old as man. Some professionals associate dependence on the extended family with schizophrenia, immaturity, passive dependency, and an unresolved Oedipus complex:

> Many middle-class humanitarians and professionals act paradoxically about family cohesion. They foster the integrity of the nuclear family, which is often pathogenic or unsuccessful, while ignoring or even being hostile to the continuity of the extended family. Thus attempts at maintaining social order are focused at only one level of social organization. Yet the maintenance of a system requires dynamic equilibrium at all levels of organization. We would hardly expect that the patient would be saved by a physician who restored the chemical equilibrium of cells while he severed the connections between organs (Scheflen & Ferber, 1972).

REFERENCES

Scheflen, A. and Ferber, A.: "Critique of a sacred cow," *The Book of Family Therapy*, ed. A. Ferber. Science House, Inc. 1972.

Commentary: Philip H. Friedman

It seems that the way the family defines a problem is very important, even when the problem focuses on a sexual relationship between a mother and her son or between a father and a daughter. In some of the examples mentioned in Dr. Sholevar's presentation, an incestuous relationship between a father and daughter which led to pregnancy did not lead to a major disruption in the life of the family. In fact, in one case the teenage girl was sent off to the grandparents, and an abortion was subsequently performed. The family apparently continued to function fairly inadequately thereafter. In other words, a family rule was not clearly broken and the violation of a strongly held norm was not enough to precipitate the fragmentation of the family. The role the grandparents played in the development of the sexual relationship between the father and the daughter was only briefly mentioned, but this factor should not be overlooked as one causative variable. Only in one example given, when a mother actually found her daughter in bed with her husband, did intense family disruption occur. In this case, a strongly held family rule or norm was apparently violated.

It is interesting that incest does not occur *more* often in families than it does. In clinical practice I have seen many families where the father and his daughter have a very close, sexually enticing relationship, while there has been no sexual activity between the father and mother for years. Incest, however, does not occur—and one wonders why. Incestuous behaviour occurs considerably less frequently in middle-class families and substantially more often in lower- and upper-class families. My hypothesis would be that there is a very strong incest taboo in the middle-class family even when marital incompatibility is very high and the sexual frustration is almost intolerable. The husband may have an affair with another woman, or some form of symptomatic behaviour or family disruption may occur, but incest will not occur.

In general, however, incest probably does occur much more frequently than statistics reveal. In many cases, it does not seem to be very disruptive to either the family or to society. Often the therapist only hears about an incestuous relationship from five to twenty years after it has occurred, when a client who seeks help for another reason mentions that she had a sexual relationship with her father. Rape would appear to have a more immediate disruptive effect on both the family and society than does incest.

Commentary: Dr. Maarten Sibinga

One of the classical examples of incest, the case of Oedipus, "the one with the swollen feet" has of course given psychiatrists much food for thought, especially after Freud's elaborations on the theme. This has led to the familiarization of the educated—and not-so-educated—public with the "Oedipus complex."

More recently, attention has been called to the experiences of somato-sensory deprivation and immobolization nature of the young Oedpius, who in early infancy had his legs tied together and was left deserted at a mountain site, only to be found and from then on to proceed to fulfill the oracle, killing his father and marrying his mother. The punishment of further sensory deprivation, his blindness, is familiar to everyone.

Dr. Sholevar expands the territory of family therapy in a very obvious and logical direction by addressing the problems of incestuous families. His view of incest as another of the many possible aberrations of sexual relations within a family introduces important therapeutic potential in a situation which often was managed with disastrous consequences to family members. Oedipus himself is a case in point. In terms of more long range prognosis for such families the old method of treatment which Dr. Sholevar referred to probably solved nothing for any member of such families. This is why follow-up studies or reports are not readily available in the literature.

It is of importance to realize that while the three families presented by Dr. Sholevar are "lower-middle-class" families, incestuous solutions to sexual problems within a family are by no means restricted to such strata of society. This was long ago pointed out by Sophocles.

The value and pertinence of inclusion of all members of the family in the therapeutic approach is well illustrated and the legal implications cannot be underestimated.

Commentary: Virginia Satir

Two thoughts came to mind during Dr. Sholevar's presentation. It is probably true that there are fewer sons who impregnate their mothers than there are fathers who impregnate their daughters; however, this does not necessarily mean that the same dynamics are not operative but simply that the sons most likely operate outside the family.

The other thought is that I have had the experience of working with a lot of girls who had been the sexual partners of their fathers, and there was an overwhelming sympathy for the fathers: "I could not stand the way my mother treated my father."

6

Changing Female Sexual Values and Future Family Structure

SYLVIA CLAVEN

Implications for Family Treatment

ANITA LICHTENSTEIN

Author's Comments

CLINICIANS HAVE LONG been aware of the necessary reciprocity of theory, research, and practice but have generally ignored this basic tenet in their daily work. The resultant loss to both knowledge of human behavior and to the client cannot be measured with any precision and is open only to speculation. A current social phenomenon, however, makes it vital that this traditional pattern in clinical practice be reassessed: This is the factor of social change. American society is experiencing a period of rapid social change which affects the therapy milieu and is directly pertinent to family therapy.

What follows is an attempt to show that change in female sex-role behavior and consequent change in the social expectations of the female have great impact on family structure, perhaps greater than on any of the other major social institutions. For some people, a period of transition in values creates inner conflict. Juxtaposition of traditional values and emerging newer values means that the individual must find his way without institutionalized normative patterns to guide him. In other words, for some, the desire to do what they have been taught is "right" is incongruent with the dictates of the world in which they find themselves. The stress thus created may be great enough so that therapy is sought. When inner conflict is expressed in family terms, it is necessary that family therapists understand the social parameters that help define "normal" and "pathological."

For the practitioner, this means that the client be evaluated within the context of the client's normative social milieu. If the goal of therapy is to help the client toward a coping or functioning level, then it is critical that the practitioner be able and willing to recognize and deal with the more universal psychological processes as contrasted with particularistic behavior. It could be said that the practitioner must be aware of the several real worlds that constitute the current social scene in order to first assess dysfunctioning, and second, to apply general theoretical knowledge of human behavior where dysfunctioning exists.

Of the many attributes of successful practitioners, two should be emphasized. First, respect for the client takes on new importance. The clinician is charged not only with the need to be knowledgeable about a client's conscious world, but with the need to respect the legitimate options he has in that world. Second, the clinician is called on to be accepting of what is normative for his client. Respect and acceptance may be difficult to achieve where attitudes, values, and beliefs are in conflict with those of the therapist. In sum, the role of the therapists is that of *translator* of a culture and not that of transmitter of culture.

The following chapter is a recapitulation of one program in the 1971 Conference sponsored by the Family Institute of Philadelphia. The discussions are an outcome of the authors' desire to demonstrate the feasibility of interaction between theory/research and the applied discipline of family therapy. The first section attempts to examine some current factors that affect the relationship beween changing female sexual values and future family forms. The second section is a discussion of ways in which these changes are manifested in persons seeking help and possible approaches to their problems. The third section is a presentation of data in the form of personal response from nine young women to the question "What does female sexuality in today's world mean to me?" The panel of women

was selected to partially represent the broad spectrum of normative female sexuality patterns observable today. Their comments
are presented as they occurred, with only slight editing, in hope
of retaining some of the impact experienced by the audience at
that session. The authors leave it to the reader to systematize
the data into some continuum ranging from traditional to avant-
garde before coming to the summary analysis.

CHANGING FEMALE SEXUAL VALUES AND
FUTURE FAMILY STRUCTURE

Sylvia Clavan

We have all observed and perhaps experienced various effects
of rapid change in many facets of modern social life. Among the
social changes often mentioned is the phenomenon freqeuntly
referred to as the "sexual revolution." The concept of a sexual
revolution most often refers to the changing sexual attitudes,
beliefs, and behavior of members of a society. What is not so
often mentioned along with this is that any analysis of patterns
of sex in society is incomplete without considering their relationship to marriage and parenthood. To put it simply, any analysis
that deals with change in sexual standards is also dealing with
change in norms determining family formation. Traditionally,
sexual behavior has always been viewed as an adjunct to existing
family structure. It is always described as premarital sex, marital,
extramarital, and at times, post-marital. In addition, all defini-
tions of sex behavior as conforming, normative, deviant, or
changing are based on social expectations of the male and female
fulfilling their roles as part of a nuclear family unit or in anticipa-
tion of creating such a unit.

A challenge to this long-held view of normative sexual behavior is currently discernible. The challenge is taking shape in
the form of increased feminism. It appears to derive two factors
connected with the Women's Movement, both relating directly
to change in family patterns. First, there is a specific suggestion
by some women in the movement that women will never be
free until the traditional family unit is restructured. Second,

there are increased efforts by women to achieve a single standard of permissiveness in sexual relationships.

The first suggestion could perhaps be characterized as an extremely radical stand. It is usually associated with demands for an end to the traditional patriarchal family. It is not a new idea. In the past, demands for an end to the family unit as we know it came mostly from politically oriented feminists who saw liberation of woman as but one step toward a total restructuring of society. While some groups in the current Women's Movement still profess this view, it is probably not true of the majority who see their primary goal as improving the status of women. The second factor, however—the trend toward a single standard of permissive sexual behavior dissociated from its family framework—could possibly achieve the same end as that demanded consciously by more politically radical women.

In general, American sexual behavior is characterized by its double standard. By this, we mean that there are different normative expectations for each sex in sexual relationships. For us, this could be translated into permissive sexual expression for males, but prohibition of such expression for females. In the 1950's, it was recognized that a stringent interpretation of this prohibition gave way for many to what Ira L. Reiss (1960) called "permissiveness with affection." That standard implies that the double standard still holds, but some exception can be made for the female if she is in love or engaged. Reiss described this category as a *transitional double standard.*

When people refer to the double standard, they are usually referring to premarital sexual relationships. However, it has also been in effect within the marital relationship. Kate Millett (1970) spoke well to this point when she said, "When chastity is prescribed and adultery severely punished in women, marriage becomes monogamous for women rather than men. . . ."

Women liberationists, and all women are feminists to some degree, feel that equality in sexual relationships is desirable. There is some evidence to support the idea of a trend toward a single standard of permissiveness. The change in sexual behavior of women over the years is rather dramatic. In one major overview of increasing rates of premarital coitus for women, the rates for 1890 and 1899 were found to be 27 percent; between 1900 and 1909, 51 percent; and 56 percent during the decade from 1910 to 1920 (Reiss, 1961). The greatest change seemed to have occurred after World War I. Those figures were accepted into the late 60's when another study, a small one, suggested that another increase had occurred between 1958 and 1968 (Bell & Chaskas, 1968).

Change in sexual behavior for the married female can also be discerned. In earlier periods, it is well known that women were barely considered in the marital relationship. A dramatic turn-about inferred when we consider the concern in recent years with sexual fulfillment within marriage. Some have referred to this emphasis as the *orgasm cult.* It might be worth noting that generally, while attitudes toward and social expectations of the female in her sex role have been changing, expectations of the male have remained relatively stable. One exception that might be mentioned is that newer demands on the male emerged from the *orgasm cult,* so that for some, expectations of the male in a sexual relationship have changed.

Although it is not possible to state with any certainty how far we have moved toward a single standard, the social climate may be ready for it. This is suggested first by the fact that there is a growing acceptance of a broader range of sexual behavior patterns. Second, there has been recent interest in the idea of an androgyenous role system. By that we mean that interest is centering on the fact that sex differentiation may be biologically determined, but attributes of gender are culturally imposed. This blurring of clearly defined male and female roles has met with both positive and negative responses. Evidence of a growing acceptance of more permissive sexual behavior can also be found in public display of sex in the movies, theater, and other mass media. In some instances, it could almost be said that sex is becoming a spectator sport! Most important, perhaps, is that the high level of tolerance of varied sexual behavior is supported in American society by the fact that sexual behavior is considered a personal matter.

Acceptance of a single standard of permissive sexual behavior as a social norm requires that the traditional family structure make some accommodation. We cannot predict what that accommodation will be. However, if we consider the present a transitional period, then we may already begin to observe some implications for family living: Young people have been experimenting with family life styles. For the future, this might mean alternative modes for child rearing. Maturing during this period of transition presents young adults with a lack of cultural normative prescriptions for sexual behavior. This means that there is no adequate model for those inclined to move toward newer ideas. Such a situation is described by the concept of *role-handicap*. For the more traditional minded, there could be a tendency toward role confusion.

The parent generation is involved in the problems of a transition period as well. The greatest press for change appears to have come from young persons of the middle and upper strata— those very groups whose families have been described as highly child-oriented. Many have observed or even experienced the pain or stress—the effects of a drastic change of values in the young from those of the parents. It is one dimension of what is meant by the term *generation gap*.

It could be argued that even the older population is involved. The already weakly institutionalized social role for Americans over sixty-five may not get better since discussions of new family forms rarely include a generational factor.

It is not possible to predict with any certainty what changes in American family life will take place. As changes in traditional, strongly held family values become visible, it is possible that greater tolerance of alternate life styles will also occur. This would help moderate effects that seem drastic in a climate of rigidly held norms. Whatever these changes may be, we can hope for and work toward providing a nurturing ground for greater development of human potential. The fact that change is taking place is particularly significant for the family therapist who is called on to help those troubled with conflicts generated by these changes.

IMPLICATIONS FOR FAMILY TREATMENT

ANITA LICHTENSTEIN

The concept of therapeutic responsibility is not popular because it introduces the personal factor of the therapist as a significant part of the therapeutic process. Family therapy, or any therapy, is at this time in existential crisis. Those who come for clinical help are hurting, vulnerable, and frightened. The process can threaten a family's life style, its value system, its generational mystique. Pressures for drastic changes are both an impetus toward constructive growth and a threat to stabilizing traditional ties, continuity, and family security. The therapist must keep one eye on questions that represent psychological conflict, and the other on clues to his client's outer social reality. Failure to heed both may introduce unfair biases and perpetuating prejudicial myths into the clinical hour.

Recently, I had family interviews which centered around a teenage daughter who was disavowing her parents' moral and cultural values regarding sex. At least, this was the presenting problem. My own personal value and cultural belief system reflects my status as a member of the parent generation. Thus it is often necessary to sort out my own generation's biases so that they do not become part of empirical observations of behavior patterns brought to me. In a broader sense, one must "hear" what the present generation is saying by observing and recognizing their peer perspectives and norms. Only then can one family's unique problems be confronted with some degree of objectivity. The presenting problem in this family can be analyzed in manageable concepts when underlying struggles are understood. The family is exploring conflict around individualization, around gaining separate identities within some negotiable value system, around getting dependency gratification without paying too high a price. For the young adult, high price often means meeting parental demands to be like them. Where newer social behavior is brought to view and accepted as legitimate alternatives, the family reaches a position where they can negotiate their own terms for growth.

Therapeutic responsibility involves, among other things, questioning the concept of "pathological," perhaps even frequent redefinition of what was earlier held to be pathological. New attitudes about sex are emerging concomitantly with new attitudes about other life areas. Indeed, neither can be viewed independently of the other. As these new attitudes take hold, we can see them translated in terms of a variety of experimental relationships between young men and women.

Developmentally, the family is modified to accommodate newer arrangements entered into by young men and women. Negotiation for commitment to child-rearing may have to operate within more flexible boundaries. Women can be expected to have different expectations about fulfilling their needs as sexual beings. It is probable that their daughters will be socialized to emerging norms and values rather than to traditional ones. Young women today will have a broader range of socially acceptable life styles from which to choose. One can even hope to see a gradual closing of what has come to be called the generation gap.

Meanwhile, these predictions raise important issues for the therapist working in a transitional era. How do our own values and experience of ourselves as individuals influence our clinical approach? What prejudicial notions need be questioned? How scientific are our published attitudes toward the psychodynamics of sexuality in the light of present social thought?

The following excerpt from a paper published by a prominent analyst illustrates my professional concern in this area. (The italics are mine.)

> . . . A basic *feminine* need is to be wanted, recognized, and above all, loved; a basic *feminine* anxiety is that these needs will not be met, that she will be deserted, abandoned, rejected or humiliated. Although *men* have similar needs, they are not present to the same degree; instead there is more emphasis on the need to be admired for power, strength, and capability. This *feminine* need and its attendant anxiety originate in the early months of the mother-child relationship, and if not sufficiently resolved, certain personality traits and symptoms develop, among which may be promiscuity in adolescence. Normally, a *woman* is more sensitive to real or imagined hurts than a *man* . . . (Herskovitz, 1969).

It is not necessary to go into an exhaustive analysis of inconsistencies and misconceptions conveyed by the above quote. I use it to demonstrate how professional understanding can be contaminated by value judgments. Do we really still believe that a mother-child relationship in the earliest months generates differential results by sex? Is it possible to think in terms of *human* needs rather than needs varying by malehood or female-hood? How self-fulfilling are our psychodynamic inferences as we perpetuate them in our clinical hours?

WOMEN'S PANEL RESPONDING TO QUESTION, "WHAT DOES FEMALE SEXUALITY IN TODAY'S WORLD MEAN TO ME?"

FIRST PANELIST

I am twenty-four and am currently working in the field of mental health. I have a B.S. in Social Welfare. I have a two-year-old daughter, and I have been separated from my husband for about a year and a half. One of the main conflicts I faced as a single parent was having to move back to my own parents' home. Being a parent and a child made me so unhappy that I decided I would move to a place of my own. This meant finding a job and also finding a woman who could be a mother-substitute during the hours I worked. I had a lot of difficulty finding a job because prospective employers felt I would not be able to commit myself to a job with total responsibility for a young child. I finally did get placed in a job that is stimulating and is helping me to grow professionally.

I did find a woman to take care of my child, but I still am faced with conflicting feelings about my responsibilities as a mother and wanting to establish an identity for myself—to be independent. It is working out all right except that I do find it hard sometimes to find time to be a mother, to handle my full time job, and also to have enough time for myself.

SECOND PANELIST

I am a junior in Social Administration at a local university and have been married a little over a year. My husband and I live in a commune, and we have decided that this is the style of life we want to continue. We cannot imagine living by ourselves again. If we have children, we want to raise them with other people so that they have role models other than ourselves. We both want careers, and that presents many problems we have not worked out yet. We think living communally may help us with those plans. Another positive thing about living communally is that I do not like the role of housewife and he does not like the role of househusband. We think living this way will help a little.

THIRD PANELIST

I am a senior in the religion department at a local university. I am not exactly sure what to tell you about myself. I was married for about nine months and am currently in the process of divorce. I would like to say about that experience that at this time I have never been happier and more at peace. My family has adjusted quite well to the idea. I am the oldest of nine children, and I am no longer living back home. I moved in with some friends. The most important thing I have to face in relation to my family is what they taught me about my sexuality. My background in parochial schools and two years in a Catholic college, and the things my parents taught me from their Catholic background, makes it hard for me sometimes in light of what I am discovering about really being a woman in today's world.

FOURTH PANELIST

I am a senior in a local Catholic college and have lived at home all my life. I will probably continue to live at home until I marry because I cannot afford to move out. I have had a Catholic background and do not regret it. There are a lot of things my parents and I do not agree on. I would say that they are rigid Catholics. There have been conflicts, but thanks to my two older sisters, I learned a lot. It has worked out very well. I get along with my parents. I do have respect for what they have to say. When we disagree, we state our feelings.

There is no feeling that I have to obey every word they say. They realize that I am beyond the stage of being told what to do and consequently, it is not bad living at home. Both of my sisters are married. Being the only one left makes it a little lonely sometimes, but all in all, I still enjoy being at home.

FIFTH PANELIST

I am a senior at a local university in the School of Education. I have lived at home all my life because my family could not afford to send me away to school. I am the oldest daughter in my family, but I have the newest ideas; the others have all been pressured to conform to my parents' standards. Training to be a teacher seems like a traditional choice for a woman, but school has helped me to question things more.

I am going to be married in June. My future husband and I are trying to plan things to fit our individual personalities rather than counting on a relationship that you usually find in marriage. One thing is that I really plan to pursue a teaching career rather than just making it something to do until I have children. My future husband and I get along well. We are both home-oriented and we have decided that we will divide our roles. He is a teacher also and will be able to be home more than most men. He likes a well-kept home and feels we can share this responsibility. We hope we can relate to each other as people with individual needs—not just as husband and wife.

SIXTH PANELIST

I am an occupational therapist and am currently working at a state hospital. I feel really compelled to comment that I respect your hopes and aspirations; I wish you good luck. I have been married for three years, and my husband is in school, so I am supporting us. He is at home a lot, and we have been trying to work out this bit about cleaning, etc., but it is difficult because first, he is not that interested in a clean home and second, he has a lot of studying to do.

When I think about what you said, it is hard for me to decide exactly what I should talk about. I really represent someone who has to do with more than one parental generation: My in-laws are quite elderly, and my parents are fairly young. My husband and I have found it very difficult to adjust to our differences in attitude since our backgrounds are very different. Because my husband decided to go to professional school, we had to deal with several different attitudes about who should support whom and whether or not women should have a career, who should do the housework, and how long you should work and wait to have children. I have really been surprised at the changing attitudes of my in-laws who were originally rigid and disapproving of our decisions. They have had to adapt to many ideas which were foreign to them, and they have been flexible and willing to say how their values are not suitable to our needs. They have a daughter who is much older and who married right after high school. She has four children. She has expressed some regrets at this.

We have felt some pressures, however, from both sets of parents who do have different values. Very recently I made the choice of taking a much more responsible job. It meant that I was obviously putting family plans off again since my husband is about to graduate. I was very surprised at the similar reaction between both sets of parents who said they congratulated me on my new job but wanted to know how long I planned to work. It seems that even more liberated attitudes vanish when grandchildren do not appear. I really want to have children, too, but I have to make the choice of when, how, and what I want to do about it. It is very hard to deal with this conflict. It is really not the pressure, but the attitudes I get from my parents and in-laws that make it hard, just when I am also struggling with my own feelings about what I really want to do.

SEVENTH PANELIST

I am a housewife, married for three years, with a seventeen-month-old son. When I was first married I could not wait to become a mother and accept responsibility for a homelife. But now that I have this responsibility and am staying home all day,

I would much rather be out in the working world— and also go back to school and be training. I find being a mother and staying home is very boring. There is nothing to do except watch television, do the housework, and play with the baby all day. My friends who are in the same spot feel the way I do. We compare opinions, and we would all rather give the responsibility of being home to someone else. Our husbands take a lot of things for granted, such as that being a housewife is very easy: All you do is get up in the morning, dress the kids, do the work, then sleep all day long or read books or watch soap operas. They do not know that you do not play, that you are occupied all day, that there are a lot of things and responsibilities to being a mother and being home. None of our husbands seems to understand why we get so bored and depressed with staying home.

EIGHTH PANELIST

I am a junior in college. When I was asked to come to this meeting and talk about my sexual role, the first thing that came to my mind was the first time that I remember being aware of being a girl. I think I was about five years old, I was in kindergarten, and I dropped out because they would not let me wear long pants. Actually, I was a tomboy and I was used to wearing dungarees all the time, so I left school. My mother did not mind because she had to take me and pick me up. When Easter and Spring came, and I was out all the time, she convinced me to go back to kindergarten. The important thing is that they said I could wear pants, that kind of changed everything. My mother says to me now, "Debra, dear, ever since then you have been a problem."

I think now that I am twenty-one-years-old, I am just beginning my life as a woman. Before, I was always aware of roles because of being a tomboy and being better at most sports than most boys. I did not know whom to beat and whom not to beat, but I think I always felt that I was avoided. I was able to perform, so when I was a child it did not matter. When I played with my brother's friend, I was just another player. I was always the steady quarterback or something so I would not get hurt. It was always apparent to me that there was some role I was not fulfilling because I knew that I was not my father's little girl, all dressed up in pink dresses and bows. I was his little girl who wanted to go out and play basketball and things like that. I am much more aware of roles now because I never wanted to be part of a role. I think a lot of it had to do with my parents letting me be free to choose my role; my parents never forced me to be different from what I seemed to want. My mother always said, "I bought you Lisa dolls, and I also bought you baseballs because that is just the way you were." Nobody forced me to be the cute little girl in the traditional bows and things. So now I am glad that I was raised that way because I am much stronger in my own differences. Except that now in a world of changing values and women's liberation and consciousness raising, I think a lot about the sexual role. I find that the change is refreshing. I have more friends now, and a lot more girls do not mind when I play hockey instead of going to a sorority house.

NINTH PANELIST

I think the identification which would describe myself to you and would make my feelings most clear, is that I am a woman who is firmly committed to the movement; in fact, I am presently working full-time in the women's movement. I have some funds to help me sustain my activities there, and I also would like to say to the panelists who are housewives that there is a really far-out article called "The Politics of Housework" (Mainardi, 1971) that I would recommend to them!

To make my position most clear in helping you to understand how one woman came to the women's liberation movement and how she has changed in it, I will cite the change in my own life expectations, particularly in the last year and a half, and to some extent for about a three-year period. I dropped out of school several years ago and began a career working in political groups— not the Democratic or Republican Party—but in the anti-war movement and civil rights struggles of the middle 60's. I always thought of myself as a radical woman who would be married to a radical man and have children, and that the way that my politics would be expressed would be to find the most radical man I could and express myself through him in a continuing way: This would represent my not copping out and not becoming a middle-class housewife. I do not know exactly how it happened, but about a year ago I began to think about the women's movement. The beginning period of my involvement in the movement was done because I wanted to be a better woman so I could find a better man. My definition for becoming stronger and more independent was that I was not going to become a passive, clinging woman. No good man would want such a woman anyway, and in a sense, my participation in the movement was preparing me in more thorough ways to be a perfect wife. I began to talk of not wanting to be married, but I think I was still envisioning the kind of relationship between men and women that marriage involved, even though the words were different. The basic feelings were the same. Somehow that all changed at some point in the women's movement, and I began to be in the movement for myself. It began to have repercussions, very heavy repercussions in terms of my relationship with men because most men were not willing to deal with my involvement with the movement. In that matter, I really had to decide whether this was going to be for me or for them. Then at some point it began to be for me and my sisters and that is not an abstraction for me. It is a sense of building a community for people who can take care of each other in the fact of the kind of hostilities that women encounter in the world when they start to talk like independent human beings. A lot of the audience giggled during some things that were said on the panel, but they were very serious ideas. A woman who stays home all day and who is responsible for taking care of the house and asks the man to help her is not embarking on a silly little task. She is embarking on what can lead to great consequences in terms of the way he looks at her and at the way she looks at herself. When one panelist talked about being a tomboy and wanting baseballs, many of us remember the punishments and humiliations when we asked for the same things. However, I felt I was a strong woman and an independent woman at an early age. If that feeling were encouraged, rather than repressed, I think there would be fewer women sitting before you in your offices asking for help because they would be able to achieve for themselves what they are as people.

Finally, I would like to say that I represent only one part of the women's liberation movement. Nobody can speak for all the women who are in the movement, and no one can speak for all women who are seeking independence, but I do feel that a sizable number of women like myself exist who have a kind of flexibility and mobility which is both economic and because we have not become committed to families early in our lives. We are really trying to change our lives in a deep way. The only implication I can see for these women in terms of family therapy would be a very heavy one for therapists, because we are beginning to believe that families are not going to exist in the same way for us. Nor does it mean that this is going to change quickly in society as a whole, but we are certainly going to be talking more and more about these kinds of ideas. We do not feel ourselves to be seeking fulfillment as wives. We do not see the nuclear family as being a satisfying structure for raising people. We do not see children as being "owned" by one mother and one father. We do not see women necessarily having to live with men. I think all of these ideas should make a difference in the way therapists today think about therapy when they deal with individual women.

Summary

It is clear from these nine spontaneous responses that changing values have made an imprint on the lives of the women represented. Members of the panel were selected on a semi-purposive basis. Although no claim is made that the panel reflects a random representative sampling of young educated women, it is interesting to note that neither does any single member represent a unique case. Thus each panelist could be considered representative of a special life-style that is constituted of a relationship network of like-minded friends and/or kin.

Woman's traditional role can be broadly defined in terms of social expectations of her in familial and occupational roles and as a partner in sex relationships. For the female, this has most often meant aspiring to wife and motherhood, to being the passive recipient in conjugal relations, and to participation in the labor force, if at all, as peripheral or secondary to familial obligations. Using these parameters, the statements from the nine panelists could be described as falling within a continuum ranging from traditional as defined here, to avant-garde, or furthest removed from traditional. As in most attempts to rank, the extremes are simplest to place. In this case, the fourth panelist represents a traditional view while the ninth clearly depicts the avant-garde. The fifth young woman is a good example of being mid-point, with the others falling to either side.

The group as a whole appeared bright, happy, healthy, and intelligent. There were no overt clues to any great inner turmoil. Rather, each woman seemed to present problems and conflicts that could be looked upon as common to persons within a particular social sphere. If the life-style of any one panelist is considered the norm for her and for those like her, then each of the panelists could be said to represent "normal" for her group as contrasted to "pathological."

It seems well demonstrated that values and role expectations for women are in transition. One fact supporting this view is the unanimous acceptance of young single women living away from their parents' home. Although a few lived at home, there seemed a need either to apologize for it (as in the fourth presentation), or to explain it (as in the fifth). It is also clear that these changes will directly affect future family structure and family life. Questioning of long-held views about sex relations, plans to live communally, interest in rearing children in different ways, career commitment as a goal, delaying marriage and/or motherhood, role sharing, and indeed, rejecting the need to have a husband at all, are indicators of coming changes in our family lives.

For the clinician, it is most significant to note that the first response from the audience of practitioners was anger, disappointment, and even a certain smugness. The general feeling that the women did not talk about "sex" was seen by some audience members as an overwhelming rejection of a challenge. Yet, all of the panel members felt that they spoke to the point of female sexuality today. The message seems clear. The awe of sex per se is no longer there for the young adult population. To past generations, sex for women and female *sexuality* referred primarily to how a woman used herself biologically. To younger women, sex is only one dimension of *sexuality*, the latter including all aspects of social gender. For the clinician, knowledge, respect, and acceptance of what research and theory suggest provide the "world of reality"—the reference point against which normal and pathological may be determined.

REFERENCES

Bell, Robert, and Chaskas Jay B.: Premarital sexual experience among coeds, 1958 and 1968. *Journal of Marriage and the Family, 32* (Feb), 81-84, 1970.

Herskovitz, Herbert H.: A Psychodynamic View of Sexual Promiscuity, *Family Dynamics and Female Sexual Delinquency.* Otto Pollak and Alfred S. Friedman, Eds. Palo Alto, Science and Behavior Books, 1969, p. 3.

Mainardi, Pat: The politics of housework. In: *Discrimination Against Women,* Hearings before the special subcommittee on Education of the Committee on Education and Labor, House of Representatives, 91st Congress, 2nd Session, Part I. Washington, U.S. Government Printing Office, 1970.

Millett, Kate: *Sexual Politics.* New York, Doubleday, 1970, 122.

Reiss, Ira L.: *Premarital Sexual Standards in America.* New York, Free Press, 1960, 83-97.

Reiss, Ira L.: Standards of sexual behavior. In *The Encyclopedia of Sexual Behavior,* A. Ellis, and A. Aberbanel, Eds. New York, Hawthorn, 1961, 999.

7

The Influence of Changing Roles On the Sexual Relationship In Marriage

Ilda Ficher

T HE IMPACT OF changing sexual roles on contemporary homelife can either lead directly to marital discord and breakdown or to marital accord and fulfillment: The "sexual revolution" can indeed revolutionize the modern marriage. Therapists constantly read and hear about the Women's Liberation Movement breeding sexual difficulties and marital discords which may ultimately break up the marriage relationship. Yet this new freedom movement should be viewed as a positive force in the home which stresses the positive aspects of raised social and sexual consciousness on the marriage relationship. The liberated wife or husband, in many cases, can free a marriage from the rigidity that stagnates both partners into passive or aggressive roles which ultimately destroy the marriage.

One of the primary ways in which the Liberation Movement's "free-to-be-you-and-me" attitude can be a positive force in the home is in the area of sexual realignment. As a result of the past fifteen years of social upheaval, married couples tuned into the sexual revolution are seeking more from their marriages sexually. But difficulties arise when these unrealistic sexual expectations conflict with the reality of an inadequate sex life. This may be reflected in a totally unfulfilling interpersonal relationship within the marriage. One of the most destructive elements that can be seen within the marriage relationship is anxiety over sexual performance. Poor performers worry about their sex life, or lack of it, and about whether their partners regard them as adequate outside as well as within the bedroom. Although these are changing times, society is still structured so that passive or unaggressive men feel insecure about their masculinity if they do not fit the traditional aggressive stereotype. Tough, strong football players are still today's folk heroes. Sexually, if the male is not the aggressor or the initiator of the "action," he will not be considered a "real man." The female is the one who is expected to be passive, submissive, and undemanding; otherwise, she is not considered a "real woman." Even if these rigid passive/aggressive roles are being reevaluated in some quarters, they still play a large part in the sexual/marital relationship, particularly in the lower socioeconomic groups where marital sex is generally regarded as a duty rather than a pleasurable experience for both partners. Although sexual attitudes are rapidly changing in the middle-class population, the majority of marriages, particularly in the lower socioeconomic groups, are still constricted by the double standard. In lower classes, intercourse remains the male prerogative; the woman's role in marriage is to please the male by "putting up" with sex and dutifully bearing children. Unfortunately, the traditional inequality of the double standard mentality, the attitude that men can enjoy sex within or outside the marriage, but women cannot, is a prevalent notion among socioeconomically disadvantaged couples, and is one of the factors most resistant to change. The enormous self-gratification and reinforcement of the self-image which pleasure during sexual intercourse affords is still largely unknown among such couples.

However, when roles are reversed and the wife is the dominant aggressor of the passive male partner, constant friction may also cause personal or marital breakdown. Many wives have become more assertive and sexually demanding. Especially during the last decade, they have had more sexual experience before marriage and often expect their husbands to please them sexually as much as they themselves expect to "turn on" their husbands. Some husbands may feel pressured by a demanding wife and do not feel able to meet her demands adequately. They may feel that she has taken the initiative away in their sexual relationship and, as a result of traditional standards, feel less able to initiate sex or to function in their established male roles. A male who is more passive than his mate may possess a self-image that is already somewhat inadequate or unmanly, and if his feelings of helplessness or impotency are reinforced by a sexually demanding wife, actual physical impotence or symptoms of sexual malfunctioning may result. Here the female may still expect the male to be responsible for her pleasure and fulfillment, even if she knows that he had had little sexual experience before marriage and perhaps not much after.

Unfortunately, assuming responsibility for one's partner's sexual response is a frequent source of sexual maladjustment; no man can *give* a woman an orgasm: She controls her own response. Likewise, no woman can *give* a man an erection. When both partners function successfully, it is because they have permitted themselves to experience pleasure and are thus as concerned with satisfying their own needs as their partners. The male or female whose ego is adequate relates sexually to an uninhibited, "liberated" partner and would have no problem achieving a positive, satisfying relationship with such a spouse.

However, it is the male or female of inadequate ego who feels trapped in an unhappy marriage role who tends to solve marital and sexual problems by separation, divorce, or other maneuvers which are destructive to the couple-unit. The problems often represent a combination of the basic personality problems of each partner, the societal changes in the institution of marriage, and the destructive stereotyped attitudes the partners demonstrate repeatedly in solving their problems.

The value of couple therapy lies precisely in its unique ability to relax or even change rigid stereotyped patterns in marriage: to "open the marriage up" to at least an awareness of alternatives to restrictive roles that may be self-destructive and destructive to the marriage. Couple therapy works as a forum to achieve the goal of self-liberation. Because both members of the marital unit are present, there is an attempt at communication and comprehension, and it is lack of communication and self-esteem which are so often the causative factors in a dysfunctional marriage. How people communicate (or do not communicate) is a good indicator of how they get along (or do not get along) together.

The observance has been made that difficulties in communication stem from one's self-concept and lack of self-esteem: People who lack self-esteem are often unable to communicate how they feel about themselves or others. For these people, sexual problems are frequently the presenting symptom in a discordant marriage, Sexual dysfunction in a marriage always indicates unhappiness with the present "state of the union" and must be treated accordingly. It should be made clear to the couple at the outset that there is never only one disturbed member of a marriage. Both partners must be counselled as a couple. Sex therapy has no value if the entire marital relationship is not treated as a whole.

The causes of sexual dysfunction are many and varied; as the author has indicated, faulty communication is most often the root cause. Where either husband or wife, or both, are repressed and inhibited, their poor sexual communication reflects their fear of closeness and intimacy. For many people, forming permanent relationships can be threatening, and sexual problems may develop as a result of such individuals experiencing themselves as locked into roles which cannot be changed, or to which they cannot adjust. This is found, for example, in couples who had a good sexual relationship before marriage, where roles were not defined, but which deteriorated when their roles became clearly delineated. Couples should be encouraged to establish open, clear communication at home as well as during therapy, and to state their needs, likes, and dislikes while avoiding "putdowns" of the other partner. Couples need to take full responsibility for the marriage relationship by telling each other how they truly feel about each other and about the roles each has assumed.

To open up these all-important lines of communication, the couples are instructed to touch each other to experience giving and receiving pleasurable sensations. Such touching, including genital touching, is a way of lessening anxiety and fear of failure during intercourse. By becoming more comfortable with their own body sensations as well as with their partners', couples learn the pleasure of touch and sensuality without having to worry about sexual performance. They learn to enjoy giving as well as receiving pleasure.

Mastering these techniques, each individual learns to be comfortable with feelings about genital and sensate reactions, and to communicate to one's partner the type and place of touch most sensually and sexually enjoyable. Tuning in to one's own body as well as to one's partner's body is a positive way of promoting a more intimate, close marital relationship. It is the first step in freeing the dysfunctioning marriage from stagnation and liberating the individual from the stranglehold of preconceived attitudes and past patterns of behavior which each partner brings with him to the marriage.

The two most "unliberated" couples seen by the therapist in marital and sexual therapy consist of submissive wife/dominant husband or, conversely, assertive wife/passive husband. Both couples are unhappy and perhaps guilt-ridden about roles which threaten to destroy the marriage. Both of these stereotypes exhibit learned patterns of behavior symptomatic of the "sick" marriage.

In relationships where the female is noticeably submissive, hidden aggression is being expressed in passive and devious ways and causes problems that are being repressed and causing subsequent anger. Submissive women often follow the role defined for them by society but are unhappy with this role. They are acting out what they consider an appropriate female response while actually experiencing and covering up many angry feelings. A variety of techniques can be utilized by the marriage therapist to help this wife change her role and achieve equal status within the home domain. First, the therapist can help the wife by urging her to communicate her feelings of being "put-down" to her husband. By encouraging a parent-child relationship, the therapist can foster a setting where the child-like female can grow until she gradually assumes a more partner-like attitude toward the opposite sex. The woman who is thus helped to understand her role in society and in her marriage is liberating herself toward a freer, more satisfying life. However, it is not enough to know oneself. The therapist must also tell the wife who is unhappy in her present role to *love* herself in order to achieve success in the marital relationship as well as in other interpersonal relationships.

By thus giving her permission to assert herself, the therapist tries to relax preconditioned behavior and allow this woman to accept her new-found assertiveness as a positive aspect of her behavior. This in turn allows her to free herself from fixated role demands, and to reaffirm her basic worth so that she can assume a role which best suits her psychosexual needs.

It is important to remember that strengthening one spouse entails changing the attitudes of the other, and that any meaningful change in one causes a corresponding change in the other. The therapist must help the male partner understand and adjust to his wife's new behavior so that her attempts at change will not be undermined. If he can view her new assertiveness as a positive element in their relationship, he will be better able to accept and reinforce the change. In fact, both partners can be helped to view their natural attributes as eminently desirable in supplying for each other what the union lacks. By accepting these attributes, the therapist allows the couple to view themselves and their roles more realistically.

This change in the male-female "balance of power" within the home can be reflected in a positive change in the sexual relationship. Because the repressed, submissive female is so fearful of asserting herself, she is usually unable to be sexually aggressive or even to show much physical response to sexual stimulation. Her preconceived ideas of femininity have forced her to stifle many of her feelings and suppress her sexual desires. She can neither initiate sex nor communicate her desires to her husband. But the wife who is "liberated" through therapy to accept herself can also accept her feelings as natural and desirable. And she will be able to express these feelings more openly to her husband without guilt. Thereafter, if her attempts at expressing sexual feelings are supported by therapist and spouse, chances are that they will be repeated. Once this female and her mate recognize that sexual aggressiveness is not the opposite of femininity, nor detrimental to acceptance by others, the physical and psychic gratification that follow should guarantee its continued use. Thus, the truly "liberated" woman is able to use her aggression more productively for her own pleasure without either guilt or loss of femininity. She will feel more desirable because she *is* more desirable as a mature woman, and this must have a positive effect on the sexual relationship.

Where the female is the dominant member, she cannot acknowledge her unconscious need to dominate and so may surreptitiously try to sabotage therapy. This type of female is also acutely unhappy in her present role: She knows society sees her as distinctly unfeminine but feels threatened by any attempt at change. She is equally unhappy with her passive mate (even though she may be forcing him to be that way). Unable to relinquish any of her power, she unconsciously feels ashamed and guilty about being so dominant.

This woman needs therapeutic support for her feelings of inadequacy. She can be helped to accept her attributes, even though they are viewed as antithetical to society's traditional norms. This is helped greatly since in terms of today's changing standards, her attributes perhaps are becoming society's accepted norm. Feeling accepted without the need for authoritarian control, this female will have less need to undermine therapy in order to escape change, and change will therefore be more likely to occur.

Again, the male's position must be given support. His assets should be stressed, and he should be helped to accept some of his passivity in a nonthreatening way. The author has found that "being comfortable with yourself" can lead to an actual improvement in self-image. This comes about when the passive male gradually assumes some of the control which his mate now relinquishes.

Couple therapy may be viewed as a reciprocal process directed toward simultaneous adjustments of each spouse to new role changes in the other. In this way, the individual satisfaction of each partner increases as does the ability to relate to each other both psychologically and sexually. Lovemaking techniques and positions can be varied to accommodate each partner's changing psychological needs for stimulations and gratification. This in turn can result in a marriage relationship made more satisfying through the thoughtful adaptation to changes in sexual needs.

In dealing with overly assertive and passive men and women, the therapist must show them the inhibitory effects on personal growth of rigid and stereotyped societal and sexual role behaviors. They should deal openly with the hidden issue of partner-control, and with the goal of a more realistic marital partnership. The basic worth of each individual in the unit must be openly acknowledged, and a healthy display of all roles and behaviors native to both partners accepted. The ultimate objective is achieving freedom from fixated roles and the option of choosing any role they are comfortable with.

One can see that the role differences which drive many couples apart can also bring the partners closer together. Liberated couples should learn to use their differences and role changes to increase the satisfaction they can give each other within the marriage.

BIBLIOGRAPHY

1. Ficher, I.: Sex and the marriage relationship. In: Oaks, W.; Melchiode, G., and Ficher, I. (Eds.): *Sex and the Life Cycle*. New York, Grune and Stratton.
2. Kaplan, H. S.: *The New Sex Therapy*. New York, Brunner/Mazel, 1974.
3. Laughren, T. P., and Kass, D. G.: Desensitization of sexual dysfunction: The present status. In Gurman, A., and Rice, D. (Eds.): *Couples in Conflict*. New York, Jason Aronson, 1975.
4. Linsenberg, M.: *Reciprocal neurotic pathology in the marital dyad*. Unpublished thesis, Hahnemann Medical College, Philadelphia, 1974.
5. Mace, D. R.: The physician and marital sexual problems. *Med Asp Hum Sex, 5*(2):50, 1971.
6. Masters, W. H., and Johnson, V. E.: *Human Sexual Inadequacy*. Boston, Little, Brown and Company, 1970.
7. Rice, J. K., and Rice, D. G.: Status and sex role issues in co-therapy. In Gurman, A. S., and Rice, D. G. (Eds.): *Couples in Conflict*. New York, Jason Aronson, 1975.
8. Satir, V.: *Conjoint Family Therapy*. Palo Alto, Science and Behavior Books, 1964.

8

Primal Scenery

PROS AND CONS OF DISCUSSING SEXUAL MATERIAL IN CONJOINT FAMILY THERAPY

ALFRED FRIEDMAN, JOHN C. SONNE,
VIRGINIA SATIR, ROSS SPECK

ALFRED FRIEDMAN

I HEARD TWO COMMENTS recently that related to the primal scene; a woman professional recounted that when her eight-year-old daughter asked her out of the blue one day, "Mother, how does it feel to have sex?" She was taken aback and had to think about it for awhile before answering. Another comment I heard was that a colleague was stimulated by these meetings to ask his wife whether she thought her sixty-year-old parents were still having sexual relations; this kind of stopped the wife who had not been thinking about it, and it took her a few minutes to recover and start talking. Eventually, this resulted in a very good communication.

Thus, even for therapists who have built up intellectual defenses, being caught off-guard and getting into the gut issues, into our own personal lives and how we relate within our families, is a different thing. It is so easy to sit with someone else's family or another couple and ask them all kinds of questions about how they handle sex with their children and with each other, how they talk about it and feel about it, and how they demonstrate it or act it out and so on—but it is a problem for professionals to do so in their own lives. The following comments are not just for working with patients or clients but also have relevance for the professional working on himself.

The term *primal scenery* intrigued me a bit, and I want to

relate to you a bit of esoterica of my own association, the chain of associations set up in my mind by the term *primal scenery*.

My first association was with the Garden of Eden. I think it happened partly because I was sitting in a synagogue on Rosh Hashana, the Jewish New Year, and I do not like to recite ritual prayer so my mind wanders at that time. (It's my best time of year for free association.) I was hearing something about Abraham and God, and I was thinking about what I had to say now of the Garden of Eden.

It occurred to me that the story of Genesis is the story of creation of—I was going to say—man, as it is written in Genesis, but I changed it after our earlier sessions here, to woman. Woman and man are created by reproduction by their parents, by their parents having had sexual intercourse, and this gets back to the phrase *primal scenery*. Now, this is a new interpretation. My hypothesis is that the tree of knowledge from which Eve and Adam ate and from which they learned good and bad—this forbidden knowledge—was not just knowledge of their own sexuality, their own nakedness, but was also the sexuality of their parents, of the primal scene and the fact that they had been born as a result of their parents having sexual intercourse. So this is how I would explain forbidden knowledge, as coming from the words "to know" (the word *know* in the Old Testament stands for and is interchangeable with the meaning, "having sexual relations").

Now I realize that ostensibly the story of Genesis is just a story about how the world began and how life began, and it presumably had to start somewhere and someplace, so when I say it is a result of parents having sexual intercourse, that statement can be questioned. But after all, what behavior would be so serious or so bad as to call forth from the Lord the threat of death? Certainly not just desiring sex for themselves but, as Freud said, having incest. Perhaps it also had something to do with the fact that the parents had sex: Possibly it was related to both. Freud maintained that the sacred prohibition of incest and the resulting horror of incest originally was nothing other than the prolongation of the will of the primal father; that is, the primal father—the early father—did not want his son to have sex within the family with mothers and daughters. If we dare now to think of God as the representation of the supremacy of the primal father, i.e. the concept of God, it becomes more understandable why the Lord was perceived to have decreed death as the appropriate punishment for such knowledge about parents, sex, or incest. I do not know whether Freud or anyone else had interpreted Genesis as I have, but it is as though the fathers of old thought it was good strategy to keep their sons in ignorance. They did not want their sons to see them having intercourse with the mother and did not tell them about it, so that the sons would never get the same idea of having intercourse with the mother. Thus, incest could be avoided.

Of course, this is only a vague impression that I have, and I certainly cannot prove it, but the impression was reinforced by my next free association, which was to recall that the story of the founding of the Christian religion, which was started by the same people in the same civilization in the same part of the world as those who made up Genesis, is firmly based on the denial of sexual intercourse between the parents of the founder of the religion. Someone said earlier, "Was Jesus married, or did his mother have sex?"

Freud presented the viewing of the primal scene as uniformly horrible to the child, and his one-sided view of this may have blocked the development of more open-minded consideration of the pros and cons of parents discussing their own sexual relations with their children. The primal scene experience has been presented in psychoanalytic literature as a severe trauma of childhood experience, and often the sexual relations of the parents have been perceived as aggressive and brutal, with the father doing something harmful to the mother. Devereux has published a paper on the Mojave Indian children whom he found not to be severely traumatized by witnessing the primal scene: They regularly saw their parents having intercourse and were not traumatized by this. He believes that the commonplace nature and frequent occurrence of the primal scene experience, and the knowledge by the children that they would not be punished by their parents for looking and for their scoptophilic activities, is what mitigated against the children being upset or traumatized by viewing intercourse. The Mojave Indians also avoided incest.

It has been commonplace in our culture for many children to repress the fact that their mothers were having sexual relations with their fathers; this is one reason why we consider it a good idea in family therapy to discuss sex or sexual relationships in the presence of the children in the session. So many middle-class parents over thirty never really talk to each other about their sexual relationship, let alone talk to their children about their sexual relationships—although I have observed that they will sit and watch TV or the new movies with their children for hours showing sexual relationships. However, they cannot really talk to each other about it or about their own sexual relationships. One might well ask the question, "Should the adolescent who is trying to break away from parental influence and become more independent share his or her sexual experiences with the parents, if the parents are not ready to share their own experiences with the adolescent?"

JOHN C. SONNE

As our Conference on Changing Sexual Values and the Family proceeds, two underlying themes seem to have been set into vibration. The first is fear of infidelity, and the second fear, which is interwoven with the first, is fear of castration. With this in mind, I would like to begin by quoting a song which is take-off on "The Sweetheart of Sigma Chi."

> The girl of my dreams is the sweetest girl
> of all the girls I know,
> Each sweet caress, full of tenderness
> Fades in the afterglow.
> The blue of her eyes and the gold of her hair
> are a blend of the western sky,
> And the moonlight beams on the girl of my dreams
> She's "the sweetheart of six other guys!"

There are several therapeutic questions to be discussed, the first of which is, "Should sexual matters be discussed in family therapy?" Gerry Lincoln and I wrote about this in the book

Psychotherapy for the Whole Family in a chapter on "Discussion of Sexual Material." We gave an example of an eleven-year-old girl who said that she would be having intercourse with her father except that her vagina was too small and her father's penis was too big. She also said that she really was not jealous of her mother because she really did not have to be jealous of someone who was old and gray and had a wrinkled face. In the same family, the father, at one point when things were going somewhat better, said that he was thrilled because his wife's vagina was a little more active in intercourse—but that he also was afraid he might lose his penis in some way in intercourse. As you can see, the question of whether the therapist should talk about sex in family therapy is best answered by saying that you should be prepared to talk about it and as a therapist should not back away from it. I do not necessarily think that you plunge in and say, "We have to talk about it"; but if it comes up, you had better be ready to listen and comment.

Here I want to touch briefly on some other clinical examples. One concerns a family with a three and one-half-year-old boy named Alan who constantly protested coming to the session but finally said he would come willingly if he could say dirty words. He was given permission by his parents. Alan was a very precocious little boy, who often came dressed in a marine outfit with two guns, a badge, and a cap. He climbed all over the place as he talked. He also told how he was "alive" with his girl Annie, and how he would lie on top of her, and they would be "swimming." He was on fire between his legs but was afraid of "the alligators" that were between her legs. He would crawl in and out under chairs, emerging exhausted from talking about his birth, how he could not go through that again, and how he had had to fight off a thousand men in the process. He said he was married to his mother, tried to pat her during the session, and remarked that his father was a "fart" and that he was going to punch him in the nose and get him out of there. Alan eventually talked about his concern over who had the penises and went around the therapists and the whole family asking, "Do you have one?" etc. He insisted that his mother had a penis or at least had had one at one time. However, when mother went into the hospital to have a little baby, she had lost her penis. They had cut it off and thrown it in the ashtray. As he spoke he started rummaging around in the ashtray. He insisted that his mother was going to grow her penis back again.

Alan often scribbled something about Atlantic City on the blackboard with chalk. His mother had a habit of lying down in bed with him at night when he went to sleep, and he would wake up in his own bed in the morning wondering what had happened. Then his parents began to think that maybe he saw them having intercourse, perhaps when they were on vacation in Atlantic City. However, the mother, disbelieving her own dawning awareness, said that the boy was asleep all the time and only woke up when he wanted to get a drink of water. (Now, it so happened that at that time I had a young man in analysis who had slept a lot with his mother, and he kept telling me how he would get up and ask for a drink of water so that he could break up his parents when they were having intercourse.) Alan later went on to say that he wanted to have his penis cut off and wanted to get a bigger one like a big gun he had seen in a department store window. (It was supposed to go "from here to the wall" and so on.) Talking about all this relieved Alan's anxiety, so that he asked to sleep in a bedroom by himself, saying he was a big boy. He also calmed down and became more appropriately aggressive in playing with other children.

Another example concerns a four-generation family composed of mother, father, three-year-old daughter, maternal grandmother and grandfather, maternal great grandmother, and paternal grandmother and grandfather. The mother had had an affair for nine months and said that she had felt loved in this affair but had given it up. She said she had sought love in the affair because her husband was aloof and cool and unresponsive. We talked about this, and one of the things that came out was that the mother would have her mother, who was psychotic, babysit for the three-year-old girl. The little girl had developed a symptom of wetting herself after she saw her psychotic grandmother listening to this in the session. We asked the psychotic daughter, grandmother to come into the therapy session along with the maternal great grandmother. The great-grandmother said that her husband was dead and that she had liked him, that he had *loved* her, but it really had not been worth all the trouble of forty years of married life. She had not wanted a little girl but had wanted a little *man*. She favored her son, who was living with her, over her psychotic daughter who was sitting listening to this in the session. We asked the psychotic daughter, i.e. the maternal grandmother, how she felt about this; she answered that she did not feel at all rejected. She then added that if her daughter, the mother, had indeed had an affair, it must have been with a man who was rich because she is a "hippie" and no one would really be nterested in her. The maternal great-grandmother was trying to control the entire family—and the session—and was constantly trying to put men down. There were two male therapists in this case, and she said that one was very nice and the other was very mean; her daughter and grand-daughter went along with this, wanting to cater to the great-grandmother. It was brought out that the great-grandmother was hostile towards all men, as was the grandmother who was giving psychotic associations about snakes ("men-snakes" and "women-snakes") being in the grass and so on.

Now the little three-year-old girl, when the theme came out about women castrating men, started to act like a barber, pretending to cut her father's hair. She was acting like a little Delilah and was very sexy with the father. Here again we talked about sex as it came out initially around the mother's affair. We can see that there were ramifications of this affair that went into four generations in this family. As a matter of fact, in regard to discussing affairs in family therapy, I am surprised how often talk of an affair occurs spontaneously in the session without a cue from the therapists. Actually, it is often the therapist who is resitant to hear about such topics, doubting his own or the family's ability to handle what might ensue.

A final example may be cited of a family with an adolescent girl who had had a sexual experience of which the family was aware. The mother tried to be very helpful, saying, "Well, maybe you didn't know what happened, you might have been unconscious," and so on. Then she said, "It occurred to me that possibly it hadn't been a satisfactory sexual experience she's had, and I wanted to reassure her that you could have a perfectly normal and happy sex life making someone else happy." The mother was talking about the experience, but she was talking about it as a projection of herself. I think it is very important for us to keep in mind that "It isn't what you say, it's the way that you say it"; You can talk about sex, and it may not mean a thing, or it may mean something very destructive.

Marriage, Affairs and the Therapist's Values

The therapist's values certainly are a part of treatment to varying degrees. First of all, the therapist is not shocked or moralistic when he hears of an affair in the course of treatment. Often couples come in and either mate expects the therapist right away to be on the side of the injured spouse. Both are often quite surprised that this does not occur. Sometimes they are not just surprised, but flabbergasted and astounded, and this opens up a lot of things. I am not saying that the therapist actually encourages people to have an affair, nor does he say that it is fine, but he does not take the position that an affair is the worst thing in the world. There may be many things that are worse than an affair for some people. How it is handled and whether there is a willingness to explore its meaning and to grow from it, will determine whether the outcome of an affair is constructive or destructive.

There is the example of a patient who on New Year's Eve almost twenty years ago got drunk along with her husband and another couple in the house. Her husband had a good time in bed with the other woman, and she was shocked to find herself half-drunk and half-awake in bed with the other man. She has not forgotten this for twenty years and is still berating her husband. Another illustration concerns a patient who was quite a dominating and controlling woman attached to her mother. Her husband had had an affair that lasted for three months. Since that time, she has refused to wash his shirts. Now he will not "fuck" her anymore, and she is "climbing the walls" with sexual frustration. He tells her, "O.K., if I'd 'bang' you, you'd be healthy," adding, "This is ridiculous."

In many marriages there is an interminable struggle for power and control. The need to be "faithful" or the demand that one be "faithful" on such a basis derives from neurotic motives, not healthy ones, and can, rather than foster autonomy and love, destroy them.

It is the author's belief that a husband and wife should be free to have an affair if either one of them would like to, and I think that this posture creates an atmosphere of voluntary love in their relationship and takes away compulsion. Furthermore, if a couple agrees on this arrangement, the chances are that there may not even be an affair or that there may be fewer of them. Not all affairs are destructive. There was a couple who became involved in an extra-marital situation at the husband's suggestion; his wife and the other man had intercourse in front of the husband and the other woman. The husband became very upset. I said to him, "Perhaps if you and the other woman had had intercourse before your wife and the other man, you might not have gotten so upset," and he said, "Yes, I think so, I might have felt differently then." The discussion continued, and he saw that if the experience had turned out differently, he might not have become so upset about it and thus might not have sought therapy.

I think there are a lot of situations that probably are either transitionally therapeutic or helpful in some way, which we never hear about and never see because we see only sick people. Even if these people ran into trouble in these situations, I think sometimes you might help them try it again, with a little more maturity, and in this way perhaps get more out of it. A lot of people who try extra-marital affairs are too immature to make them successful. Here, I think, there is a paradox, in that such sexual experiences may be of a transitional nature. They may be of therapeutic value to the participants—which shows that they are looking for increased maturity—but affairs have the greatest likelihood of therapeutic success if the people involved are as mature as possible to begin with. If they get into affairs with immature people to gain more maturity, the relationship may fail because those involved are too immature. This has happened in communes where people wanted to share on all levels, including the sexual level, and they got into such a problem with jealousy that the whole commune fell apart.

Finally, let me cite a film called *le Bonheur* (*The Happiness*). The plot went something like this: The husband had a sexual affair which was very meaningful to him and helped him grow. Afterwards, he came back to his wife and said, "You know, I love you so much more, darling." After he told her about the affair and how much he loved her, she committed suicide. This may mean one of two things: That the affair was a bad thing or that it was not handled well by the people involved.

VIRGINIA SATIR

I agree that we can learn much from each other, but I am concerned with what someone learns about what he sees and experiences. I have developed something I have called *family reconstruction* in an effort to find out at a given moment what one's learning is all about. We all have "learning" that we have acquired since birth and even before that, so what we make of what we see and hear becomes really the most important question.

I do not want to use the words *primal scene* because they mean something else. If a child sees his parents in intercourse, what kind of learning is acquired? Children acquire different kinds of learning. I am reminded of a contemporary who related that when her child was four or so, she and her husband were making love in the afternoon, when the girl entered the room. There was a message in this family that they could talk about anything: whatever it was, they could talk about it. So the little girl asked, "Daddy, what are you doing to Mommy?" and Daddy said that he was making love to her and the child said, "She doesn't look very happy to me, it looks like you are hurting her." This gave the parents a chance to give this child some kind of picture of what was really going on, which she otherwise would have misinterpreted. When I think of the many people I have been privileged to reach on a gut level, and discovered the false learning that comes not only from watching parents in intercourse, or half-watching them, but other things as well! I remember when I was little how I used to peek through the bannister to see if I could see my father in his nightgown to find out what was between his legs. I did not find out for a long time.

There are many learnings that affect how one feels about himself and his own freedom. It can be the memory of a dinner table when the children are questioning and mother and father sit stiffly. (This kind of learning can be destructive.) So, for me, it is not a question of "should" or "should not," but what kind of learning is derived and how is it used? One of the things that can be done within the family in therapy is to make it possible to comment on *everything* so people know what they are hearing and seeing and what they have made out of it. For example, in working with a particular family a closeness was developed, to the point where the barriers were let down and everyone could really communicate openly. At one point, the little five-year-old said to this mother, "Mommy, why do you always carry jelly and cream cheese to bed with you?" She looked at him and looked at me and got red. She looked at her husband, he looked at me and there was a very interesting communication at that point. I had only a small hunch of what was going on. Our rapport was good enough so that finally it all came out because there had been an agreement that we could give straight answers; and it was something that I had not heard before. Before intercourse, it always seemed to be a better idea if the husband put jelly and cream cheese on his penis because it was more tasty. This led to some very interesting things! That was a more dramatic kind of experience, but we all weathered it well and even did some role-playing in the session.

It is difficult to say with any certainty what the child learned from this discussion and the ensuing role-playing. However, one of the things that this child might have learned is that there are many ways to do things, and I feel that was good.

ROSS SPECK

I believe we owe to Chairman Mao the statement that the world is in a state of perpetual turmoil and chaos, and we should get used to it. However, change is difficult for anyone to integrate. Mankind seems to be searching for some kind of Linnaean system in our human bondage. The Chinese offered an ancient classification which intrigues me greatly—a classification of animals, which would of course include humankind. (There are some advantages in *not* viewing the world according to Aristotle!) Animals were divided thusly: (a) belonging to the emperor; (b) embalmed; (c) tamed; (d) suckling pigs; (e) sirens; (f) fabulous; (g) stray dogs; (h) included in the present classification; (i) frenzies; (j) innumerable; (k) drawn with a fine camel's hair brush; (l) etc.; (m) having just broken the water pitcher; and (n) those that from a long way off look like flies.

I would suggest in our dealings as family therapists with human beings and with the chaos in our world today that the social, political, and therapeutic processes are all of importance. Liberation of human beings evolves in a multidiversity of ways. Alternatives are needed and it is not necessary that any of them be right or wrong, good or bad. Each person is entitled to choose what is best for that person as long as it does not physically hurt someone else.

Therapists are seeing a lot of new families with new kinds of structures, and they had better get rid of the notion that there is any dogmatic formula for any group that chooses to live together. The job of the family therapist is that of a catalyst, or referee, or philosopher, or someone who can provide a new idea or a bit of innovation to help bring about the evolution of whatever the group is involved in. I think people are moving into newer and larger kinds of tribal groups. Not everyone is sure that the nuclear family will be here as the primary group in a hundred years. (See David Cooper's *The Death of the Family*: For many people this book is a shocker, but it is filled with innovative ideas.)

Each family is different, with different goals depending on what they come to therapists for. At present I tend to work briefly with families, perhaps only six to ten sessions, and sometimes less than that. In some cases sexuality in the family may not be relevant to the family problem; in others it is central and must be discussed even in the presence of the children.

In many ways people are still under a cultural taboo, but in the clinical situation we have to talk the language of the people who are involved. Let me illustrate this with a brief clinical example of the need for discussing the primal scene.

I first saw a seventeen-year-old girl who was hooked on drugs, had had two abortions, and felt depersonalized. She is now twenty-one, and I have worked with her family for three years. Her father and mother would cuddle her in my waiting room, and play with her with their hands between her legs. I found that the parents frequently had intercourse while she and her brother were with them on the parental bed watching TV. She introduced the thirteen-year-old brother and also her dog, into sex. A central problem has been her lack of feeling of identity, and her fantasies are that she is a boy. In intercourse she wants to be on top, and her partner has to be totally passive. She has also been involved in orgies. Her current lover is a homosexual male who allows her to watch men have intercourse with him. It is apparent that in this kind of case we must deal with sexuality at all levels in the family and that discussion of the primal scene is essential.

ALFRED S. FRIEDMAN

Some of the things that have been said here about sex and about parental sex, that is, between father and mother and husband and wife, also apply when we talk about freedom of expression within the family and open communication about parents' extramarital affairs. One of the rules that some therapists go by is that if it comes up, or if it obviously needs to come up, or if it is already known, it should be discussed. If the children have a pretty strong hunch about it (even if they are not sure and are already wondering about it or have some doubts or anxieties about it), I would say that it certainly should be discussed. Some therapists have also suggested deciding each case on its own merits. If the parents who have the extramarital affair or affairs are not ready to talk about it and do not want to, should they be forced? In general, therapists certainly ought to try to encourage couples to face their extramarital affairs together. It often follows that it would be constructive to discuss it with the children, although there may be exceptions to this: It depends on how much discussion is needed in the individual case.

9

Symbolic Sex in Family Therapy

CARL A. WHITAKER

In the process of family psychotherapy organized towards growth in family unit and individuation, it is assumed that the greatest flexibility of role structure defines a healthy family. It is also assumed that the basic taboo in most WASP families is overt violence. To build towards work in the area of violence, it is highly useful to wander around in the family's dynamic style patterns. Such strolling, hopefully in bare feet, may increase the sensual thermostat and yield access to the warmth and sensual experience the family members share with each other. This necessitates an implicit, or better, an explicit contract with the family stating that what happens in the therapeutic setting is free of the usual taboos, and that in the exploration of sexual and sensual territory one is dealing in a kind of pilot project for the family's living together. One obvious entré is to define early who in the family are heaters and who are coolers. Usually, the most warmth is found in the youngest, and the cooling process is frequently divided between father and mother. He excuses his as "reality," and she hides hers as "morality." Our access to the heat of their sexuality should precede tickling the red hot poker of violence.

For the therapist to invade the taboo structure of the family, he must first become personally related to them so that he has an understructure of *caring* and so that his movement within the family sculpturing and the family role assignment is received as either amusing or tender or experimental. His inroad can be structured so that it is not binding if the family is left free to veto his assistance at any time. If the therapist's movement does become binding on the family, they will have no alternative

136

but to oppose it. Thus the therapist must be willing and able to withdraw any of his moves if they are too painful.

One obvious method is to use a pattern of double-talk. 'Such casualness moves back and forth from double-talk about life to double-talk about the household to double-talk about sexual excitation, cuddling, playfulness, or childishness. It is important for the therapist and the family to participate in this as a valid procedure, although awareness is not necessary and sometimes may be limiting. Nevertheless, the pressures of the acculturation process are exaggerated in the bosom of the family and further augmented by the incestuous taboos attached. It is important to recognize that, as Esslin says, "Direct input frequently only produces recognition. Real learning comes from indirect communication."* Therefore, the therapist is well advised not to talk straight but to stay obtuse and covert. Double-talk is an asset, not a problem. Double-talk can be, of course, done in many different ways. One can use upside-down-talk and say the opposite of what he means or couch it in such a coy manner that everyone knows what's behind it, or he can express the other half of his message by his disbelief either in tone or in the quality of sentence structure. Even the tone of the voice can convey the message, "This is a put-on" so that the patient and family members recognize the tongue-in-cheek quality; with some families, it is possible to set up an ongoing communication code in this double-talk as children do with pig-latin.

It is important to state also that the children being part of family discussions of whatever character poses no danger. It is my conviction that they can tolerate discussion of murder, suicide, divorce, infidelity, incest, etc. with no traumatic repercussions *if* the therapist is caring and personally concerned with the spirit of the family and if he is trying to be helpful and not simply pornographic.

It is perfectly possible to say to the wife of a husband who has been unfaithful, "Have you ever thought of competing with him? You might even go into the business and offer him a

---

* Esslin, Martin: *The Theatre of the Absurd.* Doubleday-Anchor, Garden City, N.Y., 1961.

chance to be Number One Customer at double rates!" Such undercover talk escapes no one and yet fulfills the basic tenet that the therapist should not demand confirmation or agreement, nor should he structure a war between himself and the family. The possibilities of *sexual symbolic carrying-on* are almost infinite. For example, father sits by daughter Jane who is thirteen; mother sits by son Jim who is sixteen, and the therapist says part-way along in the interview, "Jim, when did you get out of the double bed, and did Jane replace you at once? Or was there a time when mother and father cuddled up to each other?" I asked this because I wanted to see if they would ever let her go to college—or would she have to stay home as an old maid for the rest of her life "to keep you folks apart" or so daddy would not go crazy. (After all, she's thirteen.) It will only be three or four years before she has her first affair or gets married or has a sex change operation!

In just this way the therapist may say to one of the parents: "Is your husband psychologically unfaithful to you? You know, is he always double-crossing you and down-grading you in front of guests? Is he socially unfaithful? You know, does he spend any time away from home he can playing golf or fooling around with somebody else rather than you?"

One of the obvious ways to increase the sensual freedom and openness of the family is to carry on a tongue-in-cheek flirtation with one of the little children, with grandmother, sometimes with mother or, more coyly, a homosocial affair with dad or one of the boys. To make this even more useful, get permission from the spouse; for example, one can say, "Dad, do you mind if I flirt with your wife during this hour? I have the feeling she's been making eyes at me, and it's good fun and I'd. like to retaliate in kind, but I don't want you beating me up." Father, in this way, is put in a corner. He cannot say no, and it does accentuate the triangular potential of the therapeutic situation in the same way that you can say to the mother, "I hope you don't mind us boys talking about fishing or about baseball. We really won't ask you to sit quietly for long." I remember one family in which the seventy-year-old grandmother came with her hair fixed up, and I said at the end of the hour, "Grandma, you'd better not come back next time without the rest of the family. After all, abortions are still very expensive." In a strange way, this kind of innuendo is known to be silly and yet the fact that you thought of it makes it a compliment and makes it open up the family for more fun with sex.

Allusions to frigidity can also be couched in oblique terms. Does your wife turn only her husband down? Do you often feel stood up? Is she less cuddly now than in the days of yore?

Impotence can similarly be investigated: "Is your hubby becoming an old man, too tired, a real softy? Does he treat you like his sister since the second baby? He looks like he isn't dead yet, but maybe it's the male menopause! Do you ever wonder if he hates all women? Did his father hate all women? Does your wife hate all men? Did her mother hate all men? And why don't you have what it takes to get her over that? She's your wife—are you scared of her when she gets excited? Are you afraid she might go all to pieces or lose her temper? Could she be dangerous? Do you play her with caution? Do you think she's afraid, too and plays you with the same caution? You guys could never get a fire started if that's true!"

In the realm of double-talk and innuendo it is very possible when you see either a broken family in a "divorce setting" or a family in which father is dead to deliberately train the children to "pimp" for mother. One can start out by talking about how lonely it must be for her sleeping alone. Counter the children saying that they sleep with her by suggesting that that is not the same as Daddy, and why they do not help her find a new daddy? The usual pattern of a wife denying any personal life for the sake of the children, and the children trying to fulfill the role of the father in protection of their mother, needs to be attacked; it can be done openly or, better yet, with tongue-in-cheek.

"Screwed-up" families do not talk about "screwing," but it is not difficult when starting the conversation to talk about sex by using allusion rather than direct street talk. It is not hard to ask Mother if Daddy is warmer these days than he was before or "has it cooled off" between them? Was their life together fun last week? Do they dream of being married to somebody else? Does he have someone in mind?

It is also possible to ask—again with tongue-in-cheek—"Does anybody in the family have plans to be raped?" One of the other entrés to the discussion of the affective component in marriage is to talk about the horrors of a husband and wife really falling in love with each other. Being married and having children and sleeping together is bad enough, whereas if you fall in love, you are vulnerable for the rest of your life. One other way of getting at the process of sexual interaction in the family is to refer off-handedly to illegitimate pregnancy or to allude to some covert sense on the father or mother's part that one of their children is being delinquent and flip the situation by saying, "So what's V.D.? A bad cold is a bad cold." It is also possible to get at the sexual component in marriage by talking through one of the children. For example, say to the nine-year-old when the whole family is assembled, "Have you ever thought when Mother's so angry at Dad for being two hours late, does she think he's dating his secretary?" The nine-year-old says "No" and you are free to back out, but Mother and Father are left with their fantasy and may come back later with some relevant discussion or an open war.

In discussing the pattern of the family structure one can define the sensual or sexual thermostat for the couple: How it is permissible to reverse family roles either gradually, or in a particular evening, or even within the hour? This kind of role reversal can take place in the middle of a fight. One minute he is attacking and she is silent, and later the roles are reversed; just so, the roles can be reversed sexually.

One simple communication maneuver for the therapist is to share his own fantasies: Did you ever wonder if your husband was really in love with your mother? Do you think all men are queer? Would polygamy save England? How will you two avoid each other after the kids left home? Should queers raise kittens? Can a homosexual man be a fit mother? Can a "butch" be a good father? Do lesbians love their children? How can an eighteen-year-old identify a gay bar? Then what should he do with it? Should parents confess their sins to their children? Which sins should they confess and at what ages? What did Alice in Wonderland really do when she went crazy that time?

One can also take up with the family the restructuring of the Oedipal pattern by suggesting that the couple could plan to stay married by living "close" i.e. back-to-back. All it takes is another cooperative couple to have sexual relations back-to-back, and of course if one does not include sex, the cooperative couple can be the son or daughter or even, more appropriately and implicitly, his secretary can be his other mate and her children can be her other mate, or his mother can be his second spouse and her father can be her second spouse, or it can even be more coy—he can use his golf partners to form his second coupling process and she can use her bridge partners or her League of Women Voters group as her co-partners!

At times one can use the psychotherapist or his individual therapy as a symbolic other mate, or he can have an affair with his love of money. The symbolic aspects of sex can also be augmented in family discussion by converting the Oedipal triangle into the David and Goliath myth, as in those families where one spouse takes on the role of the Goliath. The other spouse, of course, then can form a coalition with the child, and gradually the child can implicitly learn to be the David that kills Goliath. This can be a symbolic killing in the sense of the teenage daughter becoming a sexual delinquent as a way of punishing the mother or father at the behest of the spouse, or it can be in much more realistic terms; one child can be brought up—a son, for example—to hate his father with such bitterness that he eventually gets to the stage of physically beating up on the father when father is mean to mother.

The symbolic significance of both sex and aggression are of less power than the quality of intimacy and physical contact in the family. Once the therapist has developed a personal sense of identification with the family his options for sharing their affect are multiple. Any dialogue with the children from three years through the teen years can center on the family pattern for livingness. The two-year-old will respond to questions about his security blanket or his teddy bear or her dolly. By five years the shyness should be melting, and cuddling or snuggling with the kitten can be expanded to include whatever parenting is available. If she has a bad dream does she cuddle in beside mommy or daddy or right in the middle of their big bed? How much does your family swap beds? Do you swap when grandma comes to visit? Who loses their bed when a visitor stays over? When dad and mom have a fight who goes down to sleep on the couch or does one of them come sleep with you? Do mother and dad cuddle in the kitchen or just in front of the TV? Who starts it? Can the kids sneak in for a group snuggle? Who's the best cuddle team—Mother and John, Dad and Mary, or John and Mary? Who likes to cuddle the most? Does dad ever come home looking lonesome or with a headache? Who plays mother for him? What, nobody? You (to the six-year-old) should always rub his back! Come over, I'll show you how (Therapist takes child behind the father, rubs father's back, and coaches child in how to massage and pummel to relieve tension), and you should always finish with a cuddle, or you could bite his ear!

One can expand the relationship of sex and aggression by getting into the problem of multiple affairs and the associated family expectations. A couple who sense their relationship is cooling often precipitate an affair. We call this a method of getting into amateur psychotherapy. They then decide by using multiple covert cues arising out of their conversation over a newspaper article, or some rumor in the neighborhood, which partner is to have the affair. When that one cooperates, the other one will later on increase the temperature of their marriage by having a fight about the affair. For example, if it is agreed that he will have the affair, that will then expose him to her, and then she feels free to hate him. He pleads guilty and then they can have the fun of forgiving him time after time as a wife does a chronic alcoholic. This may even go too far, as Eugene O'Neill has described in "The Iceman Commeth," when the alcoholic comes back into the bar and says to his friends, "Well, I finally did it." They ask, "Did what?" "I killed my wife. She forgave me once too often."

The most important component in all of this discussion of the sexual-aggressive combines in the marriage state is the recognition that the marriage system is in control, that the plans are jointly laid by the couple, and that the person who activates them is doing so under contract and by carefully agreed-upon plans. Fighting, like sex, is a gradually escalating contract with careful arrangements established between the participants by an implicit and covert, constant and accurate communication pattern. One detailed example of this is "Who's Afraid of Virginia Woolf," as beautifully described and portrayed by Watzlawich in "The Pragmatics of Human Communication." We as therapists may hope to change the escalation only if we utilize enough power to deflect the system. If we join the system and yet are not captured by it, we may use our symbolic role to correct its distortions.

10

Third Nathan Ackerman Memorial Address (1973)

CARL WHITAKER

THE TECHNIQUE OF FAMILY THERAPY

I AM GLAD TO have a chance to talk about family therapy. I have a sense that each time I talk about it, it changes me a little. First, by way of introduction, I would like to take the position that knowing is important but that sometimes unknowing is more important. I had a very exciting experience in Texas two or three years ago. I was ushered into a family interview, and the family turned out to be the identified patient, her boyfriend, and the boyfriend's sister. I had the feeling that I had been "taken" in this strange territory, with no real friends and no real sense of warmth, and I got this kind of distorted family. I started fooling around with it and after about ten minutes I decided "Oh, hell! It's a dud, I have had it and maybe this time it's a flop and maybe next time it will work." It was an though the admission of defeat to myself threw me into a state of being alive, and all of a sudden the interview became real, human and moving. I discovered ever since, that whenever I can get to that step of facing my own defeat, it seems to make a new point of departure, a new sense of belonging with and going along with what is happening, and so is the value of unknowing.

Dr. Whitaker's address at the annual meeting of the Family Institute of Philadelphia in October 1973 is published here as it complements his paper on Symbolic Sex in Family Therapy—Editor.

It is a unique and touching thing for me to be giving the Ackerman lecture. I was not quite sure about the wisdom of the community—whether I was given the opportunity because I am a nonpsychoanalytic layman type of therapist, or because I am turned on by kids; whether because in my old age I am another "dirty old man" like Nat, or whether because I am closer to death, I should know more about it. Actually, I was only professionally acquainted with Nat. There are so many people who have been intimates of his, family therapy children and grandchildren, as it were, who knew him so much better, and I feel quite humble trying to say something about Nat and his outstanding contribution to this field. He was certainly one of the seminal minds—if not the actual grandfather. When I was taking my second year of Latin, one of the examiners asked about Virgil, and I said he was the father of all Roman poets, which pleased the teacher. So I think that Nat was that. I also wondered if it was a way of honoring my Jewish inner self. I discovered some six or eight years ago that I am a disenfranchised Jew. Being brought up in the Adirondack Mountains as a good Methodist, it was thirteen years that I lived in the Old Testament. My fairy stories and murder mysteries and sex education all came out of the Old Testament. I was a good Jew and all of a sudden when I became thirteen, someone said, "I'm sorry about this, but you don't belong to them. You're out of that, you belong in the New Testament." Suddenly it turned out that I was not a Jew after all, and I was disenfranchised. (I still grieve about all that.) Maybe this is a chance where I can wiggle my way back in, by being one of Nat's children!

I would like to say something special about Nat because he was a very special person. I will list for you the things that have occurred to me. I think he was a specialist in the multidisciplinary approach. In a strange kind of way, Nat, by himself, was a group. He was a grandfather one minute, a grandmother the next, a boyfriend, a husband, a flirtatious lover; he could flip from one role to the next so fast that it would make me dizzy watching him from a distance. I never was quite sure about his homosexual boyfriend competence—I think of that as one of *my* assets—but I never did date Nat, so I am not sure how much his competence extended in that area! I think of it, by the way, as a very important area. In fact, it is one of the rules I have taken from one of my residents: "If you don't seduce the father in the first interview, you've had it." The other is that family therapy is like chess, you had better not move the queen until you have your game well into mid-phase. The residents come back time after time saying, "Hey, look, I've just lost a family"; and I ask what they did to the mother and they say, "Well, the mother and I did have a fight" and I say, "Too bad about that. Talk to your analyst about it."

Nat had a way of what I have thought of as guerilla invasion of the family. He would sneak into the family by all kinds of manipulative modes and gyrations so subtle that before you knew it, he belonged more to the family than the members themselves (which, by the way, is not infrequent). I saw a family recently in which the older son had come back from the West Coast to straighten out mom. Papa had died and mom had taken to drinking. In the course of the first few interviews, I asked him how much he belonged in the family since he had been living away for so many years, had married, and had several kids. He said he did not feel he belonged to the family at all anymore —of course he had stopped his job and came all the way back to stay for several months. I said, "How long have you been out of the family?" and he said he had never belonged in the family. So taking his cue, I went around the group, and there were several of them there, and not a single one felt he belonged in the family. Thus one of the secrets at which I think Nat was an expert was a conviction that the family was a whole, that it had a sense of unity, and that this is one of the biggest things to get underway when you first begin seeing the family. If you do not discover that it is a unit, they may not discover it. They may have been living in it for many years and have no sense of belonging to it. They just happen to be around.

Nat was also an expert in the use of power. With him it was so natural, and he had so much of it, that it was not much of a problem. But I suggest to the rest of you that you think of it as a very important part of family therapy, because, uniquely different from individual therapy, family therapy is a political process. It is really a naughty word nowadays and I am really sorry to have to use it, but I could not think of another word, so, you try to "Watergate" the family. You have to develop a sense of power that the family has, and if you cannot find your own way for taking over, you probably are not going to be of much use. Let me see if I can suggest a way of talking about it for a moment. Think of five or six people who have been living together through thick and thin, and there is a lot of thick in any family: divorces and death, fights with neighbors, attacks by the Rabbi, financial trouble, and financial luck which is almost as bad; you name it, and they have gone through it. Along comes this character who thinks that by a few extra words he is going to change their way of living and that is pretty weird. The whole process of assuming that any individual is going to walk into a group of five or six and take over is weird. If you do not think so, ask any athletic coach what it takes to handle a team to make it operate effectively or to take over from a previous man who had it operating effectively. It is a major move, it is a massive political group process, and you need to get started with some sense of how important it is for you to carry some kind of power, some kind of political knowhow. There are many ways of doing this: One of the most important and simplest ways is to do something in the beginning that makes it clear that you are going to set the rules. Everyone shows up except papa, thereupon you agree to charge them and not see them and send them back. They are indignant and refuse to come, etc. So you lose a case. You get a conviction in yourself that there is such a thing as an important father. But it is really very difficult. Margaret Mead was right when she said the father is a social accident: He just happens to be around. But in the family structure, he is a very important individual, and if you lose him, you are probably going to lose the family. That is the advantage of being homosexual or better, homosocial. So if you can work out that process of becoming a significant person in the beginning, you have a way to start. Bobby Fischer did well when he was getting ready for that chess match in Iceland. This is like that, although it does not have to be quite that devious or stress-inducing, but I think a lot of that quality is important, and Nat was a master at it.

Another important component, I think, and partly an extrapolation of Haley's notation, is that the expert therapist uses *indirection.* That really is a further extrapolation from Esslin's notation that one of the important things about the Theatre of the Absurd is that it deals by indirection: That the covert message is the one that produces change and the overt message, quaintly enough, produces recognition and nothing else. I had a very interesting experience when I took chemistry. I had a great faculty man, and the old prof himself was doing the initial lectures in organic chemistry. He moved from inorganic chemistry through the beginning of organic chemistry. I sat with my mouth open just fascinated for six weeks, and then we had an examination and I got a thirty-six. I caught on then to the fact that recognition was not enough; that somehow I had to learn that stuff! I think many times we have a sense that direct information is all that is needed to produce change. I would like to warn you ahead of time that it is usually something the family has heard thirty times before, and there are very few new things except things that will confuse them. If you can get something that confuses them, that may help. Nat was an expert in the put-on: Help the family get confused. I frequently help them sense the fact that this is what they are there for. I am not trying to get them anyplace, I am trying to confuse them so they will not go on the way they have been going. We had a bunch of nonprofessionals who were running an alcoholic rehabilitation center in Atlanta, and they finally got around to inviting the professionals in and were trying to tell us what they were doing for a few years (and doing very well). What they ended up saying was "We are just trying to screw it up so they cannot enjoy their drinking anymore." I sometimes have the opinion that is one of the important things to learn about family therapy! If you can screw it up so they cannot enjoy the way it is going anymore, they will work out ways of making a more adequate and effective methodology for living which will give them more enjoyment. There is another way of looking at this put-on, this induced confusion. I have come to call it *forced transference*. It is really surprising what happens when the family comes in for the first interview and you say, "Hello, sorry there is someone missing, can you get them on the phone?" and they cannot. You then say, "Well, we'll have to charge you for the interview, if you can get the family together call me and we'll make another appointment." "Well, aren't you going to see us?" "No." "Why not?" "The family is not here." "Well, we are all here but Joe." "Sorry about that. No family without Joe." "Well, can't you see the rest of us? Why not?" "I won't feel right about it." "Well, how about next week on Tuesday?" "Sorry about that, I don't think we should make another appointment." "Why not?" "Well, I'm not sure that you can get the family together, you didn't do it today." "Well, we'll get him here next time." "Why don't you see if you can get him and then give me a ring." In a strange kind of way, it does both things of making sure you have a "legal" contract that is going to be binding on both sides, but it also means there is going to be a whole new sense on the family's part of how important the missing member is. I think one thing this *forced transference* is—if I may be Christian at this point—is what we mean in the Christian end of this world when we talk about the Holy Spirit. It is the sense of wholeness, a sense that we are an entity.

Barbara Betz said a long time ago, and I believe it is still very pertinent, that the dynamics of therapy are in the person of the therapist, not in the techniques, not in the process, and not in the understanding.* I think Nat was uniquely adequate in this sense. As a person he conveyed a tremendous amount of power, wholeness, and the willingness to accept and face confusion, to live in a state of uncertainty. One of the things I value in myself is my endless suspicion of myself. There is almost nothing I believe in. I keep reorganizing my theories

---

* Barbara Betz, personal communication.

and each time have the feeling that this time I made it. When I was doing child psychiatry in 1941, my first private patient was a three-year-old. I said hello to mama at the door and sort of sneered at her under my breath. I took the three-year-old in my office, and we had fun and I handed the three-year-old back to her at the end. I did this for ten sessions and got a call from the father whom I had not seen or heard of and who was a physician. I did not know whether to charge him the three dollars every interview or not, and he said, "Hey, you know, that's great stuff. My daughter is much better, and it has changed my wife, and I think I'm different too!" I thought that I had found the secret of life! It has never happened to me since. So, my dynamic theories are up for suspicion.

Nat had this loving-heartedness that I think was conveyed to families and gave them the freedom to be loving, which is a hell of a hard thing to find. I find pearls as I go along, and one of the pearls for me is a small child. You can cuddle a three-year-old, you can pummel a five-year-old, you can play sex-talk games with little kids, which you cannot possibly do with parents, and it is as though you were cuddling mother or daddy, as though you were talking directly to the parents when you are just talking to the kid. You say to a nine-year-old, "Listen, did you ever think that the reason your mom is mad when dad comes home two hours late is because she thinks he is playing with his secretary after hours?" The kid says, "What do you mean?" "I don't know, I just had this crazy thought." "How's school going?" "Oh, pretty good." And you have, by indirection, left a pill in mothers and father's teeth that they cannot deny and that they cannot possibly not have heard, and all sorts of funny things happen in the next two interviews, including the possibility they will not show up. Do not hope that they will show up. Leave treatment you do not give. For example, there is a family that came in from out in the country. Father was all upset because the teenage daughter was "about to become delinquent." He probably was afraid that he was not going to be in on the fun. About the second interview, mother's passivity in front of father's panic and daughter's hostility about father's jealousy erupted into a small-time explosion. Next interview, dad said, "Hey, can we start any earlier, I'm losing work." I asked him why he came and he said, "I thought of not coming, the damn stuff is not helping anyway." I said, "You want to leave now, you will only lose a few hours." He said, "No, I think I'll stay to the end of the hour." "You know you don't have to. I'll charge you anyway." He said that since he came, he might as well stay. I said, "Mom, is it all right with you if we stop?" She said, "We just got started." I said it was a shame for dad to lose all that work. She said, "I'm not going to put up with all the stuff I have been putting up with." I said, "I don't know, he may be different if you're that way." To the daughter I said, "What is it to you?" "Hell, I didn't want to come from the beginning." "Well, are you willing to stay for the rest of the hour?" "Sure, if this is the last one." So they stopped, because it was not helping. In terms of my way of looking, it may have been the most important thing I did in those three interviews: to let them accept the failure and take the responsibility for really running their lives. It was as if the group agreed that they did not need a psychiatrist, that they were a family that would make their family work themselves, and that may have been more important than a whole mass of understanding and communication training, etc. So, I am even suspicious of my therapeutic competence!

One of the other things at which I think Nat was a master was the power of paradox. The power of the dialectic, the power of never being caught in the corner so people have to either accept what you say or fight you: This means you can always leave the inferences up in the air so that when they decide to pull them down and insert them in their own heads, they do it on their own initiative, or they can just let them float there. You are really not set with some conviction that they have to buy. In this way the family begins to gradually take the initiative for the life to live the way they want to live. Now, if mom wants to be a lesbian, and pop wants to be a homosexual, and the kids want to relax and let the world go on, I think that is their right. I have some objections to suicide because I have a feeling that it lets the implicit murderer in the family get away with murder, and I do not like that very much. Every once in awhile, a gal says after the first interview, "Do you think I should divorce him?" I have developed a stock answer (One of the problems of old age is that you get stock answers) and I say, "I'll tell you what, I've been married thirty-six years and ten months. I think I'll probably stick with her. What do you want to do with yours?"

Part of Nat's power tactics was the process of how to enter the family, which I mentioned before. There is a second component of what I think of as good family therapy, and that is how to get out of the family. John Rosen was probably a master at this. I remember watching John talking to a schizophrenic one day about how her mother's milk had been poisoned and how his milk was pure gold and she could have him forever and he would always be there, and it was really quite tender; all of a sudden he turned to the guy standing next to him and said, "Hey, Joe, let's go play golf," and walked out. The first time I saw that I could have slugged him, because I had a sense that it was not fair to treat a sick human being like this. Over the years, I have discovered it is a very important trick because if you walk in and become a Jewish mother who is symbiotically locked into the family or patient, it is no big deal. It is important to get there, but if you cannot get out, you are just like the previous one, and you do not help at all. How to get out of the family is a very important process; one of the ways I get out is to become more convinced of how absurd I am. I decided recently in the middle of an interview while I was bored and trying to think of something interesting, that God must be getting very old and probably is going to retire. When he does, if he asks me to take over, I am going to work out some plans. I have been working on that ever since. I have decided that people will switch gender every ten years. Man is going to have the first baby, and you can borrow time from those people who do not want it. We are going to have detachable penises when we switch gender. I have wanted to be a female for many years and have never made it. Maybe I can make that part of my initiation rites! Each family member is trying to individuate—in a way, to join without being locked in—and to individuate without being outside, and the therapist better know how to belong, be loving, be hurt with pain because of, cry with, and at the same time be able to back out and be separate. He should know that his life and patient's family life are different and separate. He should be in charge of when he makes those moves in and out, and this becomes more and more difficult when you get past the first and second interviews because you become as vulnerable as the family. As long as you are in the first or second interview, you can be a technician. By the time you get to the third, fourth, or fifth, you are probably a human being, and you had better watch out because you are vulnerable; they can get you, and they outnumber you and outgun you, and for me, that means I should have a co-therapist!

Now, the things I do not know about Nat are about Nat as a person. I was not given the opportunity to be close to him. But I can guess about his joyfulness, and God protect me from a family therapist who is not having any fun; if I have to take him as seriously as he takes himself, I will never make it. Harold Searles is famous for a lot of things concerning schizophrenia, but one of the things was that if the schizophrenic can get to the point of laughing at himself, he is on his way out. And I have the feeling that the same thing is true of the family. If the family can get to the point of laughing at itself, then you have made it over the top and from then on it is coasting down. I think Nat had a joyfulness that made for real wholeness. Again, let me flip into my Christian upbringing. (Someday, I am going to teach a course in schizophrenia with Christ as the continuous case study. Isaac Singer said that there are three hundred Christs in Jewish history). He said that the Kingdom of Heaven is only available if you become a little child, and Heaven, of course, is living in your own person, in your own unconscious. How do you become a child and how do you get the family to have the courage to become childlike? Part of it is playfulness. The freedom to be ridiculous, to be irresponsible. There was a couple we had been working with, both crazy as hoot owls, a "schizophrenogenic" kind of family: The daughter went off for a year's trek into Africa. She came back and really did not need the family, and went off to college, so we went on seeing the parents. They came in a few weeks ago, and the mother said she did not have anything to talk about. I said that we could go for a beer, and the resident said, "Great, let's go." So we got up and went out. We got downstairs about two or three floors, and daddy, who was a responsible physician type, said, "Shouldn't we have the interview?" And I said, "Mom, quick, goose him before he gets another thought like that." So we went over and had a beer and a hamburger and probably the best interview in a long time. On the way back, dad says, "Well, we'll see you next Tuesday." And I said, "Not me you won't," and he asked if I would see him again, and I said, "Well, I guess you can if you are convinced that it is necessary, but this seemed to be such a good way of saying goodbye that I would hate to mess it up." That has been three weeks, and we have not heard from him. The thought that they can get along without me is shattering, but several other people have too. So this is the kind of playfulness, joy, silliness I mean. One family came in for a first interview, and the problem was that their teenage daughter had "poor ego boundaries." I put a big x in the middle of a paper I was going to put notes on and gave it to her in case she needed ego boundaries. It is a way of getting out, of separating yourself, a way of showing the family how to individuate. It is really an extrapolation of that famous book, *Where Did You Go, Out . . . What Did You Do, Nothing*, which is a child's way of telling his parents to get off his back, but doing it in such a nice Jewish double-bind way that you do not know what to do with it, you do not know how to handle it. I think the therapist should learn from that.

One more step in this process, one of the other ways of finding the Kingdom of Heaven is to be crazy. About thirty or forty years ago—I am just guessing—art became crazy. Then about five to ten years later, drama and literature became crazy, then gradually, music became crazy. Science has got some crazy impulses there but it is kind of hard-put, really. I think we are now in a stage where it is all right in the world culture for people to be crazy. It is all right to break out of the linear crazy organizational, structured life that we have made the law of reason or the rational and *really* be crazy. So, I advocate that you learn how to be crazy, that you take those crazy parts of yourself and amplify them, follow your impulses, follow your irrationalities, share them with the family—and God knows the family is safe. If there is one thing true of the family, it has homeostasis like you don't have any knowledge of! There is no danger of you, the therapist, harming the family (say I from on high). The only question is whether you make any dent at all, or whether you will be just one more flea that happens to pass by. Again, I do not think there is any danger of your doing any harm. So with that in mind, you should be able to share almost anything: (I say *almost* because we used to teach medical students back in Atlanta many years ago, and one day this lady showed up with her policeman brother. The student who had been seeing her was honest and said to the girl that he would love to go to bed with her. It was said very honestly, and I hoped it was a symbolic statement, but the policeman brother did not appreciate this at all. He did not think it was symbolic. He did not think it was even therapeutic. A little bit of judgment you should use already!).

There is another tremendous value in being crazy and that is when you develop a symbiosis with a schiz-identified patient. I like schizophrenia because I think it is a disease of abnormal integrity; the people are really doing their thing, and I say it with reverence and not with any facetious overtones. I really think this is what craziness is, *abnormal integrity*, a creativity that brooks no interference. Now the problem is that most people who end up in state hospitals are also stupid. I make money out of being crazy. Picasso not only made money, he also had fun. Institutionalized mental patients should all have Picasso's kind of craziness! All crazy people have the kind of opportunity

Picasso had. If you become symbiotically involved with a patient, then you have done that because you are like the mother. You lock in and double-bind the patient, and the patient double-binds you and there you are, tied in a figure 8. The difference is that when you have been locked in like this, in contrast with the mother who is terrified about going crazy, hopefully you want to learn about how to be crazy. When you make the move into craziness, the patient symbiotically has to move into the sane position, and then you have the way for curing the schizophrenia. This is an extra pearl because as soon as this is reversible, then the patient has a new sense of his capacity to be sane, and of course you learn about the freedom and opportunity of being crazy. So these two become flexible. When the patient becomes sane, he becomes scared, so you have to stick around and teach him how to learn, and then you move back and forth.

Let me tell you a story about an eighteen- or twenty-year-old "schiz": We had been working with the family for a year or a year and a half, and the daughter had really gotten the family on the ropes. She had been screwing around all over the place and had VD several times, and this very nice family was upset. She arranged to have herself kicked out of college several times, and dad finally decides that he cannot support her if she is not going to succeed in college. She gets herself kicked out of her apartment and comes home to live with the family. She then starts bringing men in, which is all right with the family for dating purposes, but dad very carefully goes to bed saying to the boy that it is time for him to go and wakes up the next morning to find him still there. The mother then blows her stack at the daughter and says, "Out of my house, my doors are locked, you can't live here anymore." Twenty-four hours later, the mother calls to tell me that she has to let the daughter back in, so I say, "Tell her, don't tell me." So she calls up the daughter and says, "Look, I was wrong, I can't say goodbye to you, you are my daughter whatever you do, and I'm stuck with it." Twenty-four hours later I get a call from the police. The policewoman says, "We have a girl down here who came in to report a murder. She said she's been murdered." (It really did not do much for the policewoman, she really did not understand.) "I called the mother and she said for me to call you." I said, "Well, you don't have to worry about her. We have been seeing her for a long time, and she is well able to take care of herself. Thank her and send her along." She says, "Well, she wants to talk to you. Will you talk to her?" I said, "Sure," and so she puts her on the phone: "Hey, Mr. Whitaker," (which is what she always called me, part of the integrity as I'm no damn doctor to her, and it is a very complimentary thing) I answered, "I think it was awful nice of you to report the murder to the police, and by the way, if you see any more murders, would you please report them, too? The police should know about all of them." She burst into this gale of delighted laughter and says, "Thanks, very much," and hung up with a bang. What had happened was that the mother said, "I love you." To the "schiz" this means you are dead, so she had been murdered. What I had said was, congratulations for admitting the murder, and if you find anymore, bring them in because you may run into two more before the morning. This was saying, I am crazier than you are, at which point she became sane and delightfully real and human. So learn how to be crazy, but learn also to be smart.

11

The Stake of Youth in Their Parents' Sexual Practices: A Panel Discussion

MODERATOR: CARLTON ORCHINIK
PARTICIPANTS: JEAN BARR, OTTO POLLAK,
ISRAEL CHARNEY, VIRGINIA SATIR, AND
STUDENTS FROM THE UNIVERSITY
OF PENNSYLVANIA

JEAN BARR

I HAVE THE IMPRESSION that the change of values is within the younger generation rather than the older generation from what I have heard at this conference. Yet, there can also be change within the older generation. A great deal can be learned from working with young people, particularly in the last five years, and it is important to comment on this because of a plea that seems to be coming from any therapists: How do you do it? How do we communicate? This plea is from the older therapists in response to what young people are saying. Part of the problem in listening to young people is that we see or hear something and have a momentary shock reaction. When this happens, I always start to look within to see where the shock is coming from.

In a commune we once visited, when we walked in, one of the young men was in the bathroom taking a shower. He had not known just when we were arriving. To get out of the bathroom, he had to go through the living room, so he came out with a very small towel, which is all he apparently had with him, wrapped around the bare essentials. This seemed a bit unusual and after an initial pause I began to think back.

What would have happened to me if I had been caught in this situation at that age? Probably I would have stayed locked in the bathroom for the entire two hours rather than go through the living room in any state of undress! Which is the more realistic way of looking at the situation? Which is the more appropriate way of dealing with it?

I have begun to re-examine my attitudes when I get this momentary "shock reaction." I have often thought that it is *my* values that are askew, not in terms of what is good or bad, but in terms of what is realistic. I have seen and heard a lot of these "kids" really doing marital therapy with their parents. I think that if these parents and others of the older generation can really *hear* younger people, together they can learn something about how to live a fuller kind of life. It is puzzling that young people possess this assurance and know-how. They have been subjected to many of the same kinds of things as older people, but they also have a kind of strength that enables them to look at things slightly differently and not feel obligated to totally repeat what they have been taught.

CARLTON ORCHINIK

The second panelist is Dr. Otto Pollak. One of the things I have always found from Dr. Pollack is that when Otto does say something it can be repeated. By this I mean he says things which are quotable. They are put together and they make sense to many people. I believe that is a difficult quality to acquire.

OTTO POLLAK

I must express something here which I think many feel—that in the excitement of being so permissive about sex we seem to forget that people, who are our obligations, suffer with these phenomena. I wish to pay homage to the statement of one of the earlier speakers, who has brought us back to the fact that these changes are awesome and terribly painful and that we are still in the process of enriching our civilization and coming to terms with them. I would not be able to talk to you about the impact of the sexual difficulties of parents upon their children and maybe vice versa without having stated this first.

The systems concept of family life implies that when one person aches, every person in that system aches. Those who expect to find ecstasy and hope in sex are frequently frustrated. When people are so frustrated they look for compensation. When parents are unhappy with one another, they will look to their children for a measure of compensatory happiness. I presume this to be the basis of the family romance. It is not that the children reach out to the parent of the opposite sex; it is the vulnerability of the parents of the opposite sex that creates the Oedipal situation. It is the parental response. In the cases therapists have to deal with, the problem is based on marital unhappiness.

The next point is that parents must be in the position of a commitment to a further stage of development. It is their own power of developing further that must help the children to develop further. If the parents have been arrested in development, and there are sexual difficulties, the arrest of the children comes almost by identification and probably also by stimulation. There is the phenomenon of foster mothers who take children because of their own arrested reasons for wanting to have babies, and why social workers take them away from the mother when that stage has run its course. Now, opposed to what people say about the consistency of the libidinal object, I would say that most children growing up in families other than foster families are not so fortunate. They have to stay with their parents beyond the real or educational level of parental arrest.

CARLTON ORCHINIK

Now we have our prime university panelists. Perhaps they will identify themselves.

WAYNE

Before we can discuss whose stake it is, youth's or parents', we have to look at the type of structural changes which have occurred and which every one has to adapt to. There has been some discussion about the changing role of women. This is one of the more sociological structural changes. However, what we have not talked about is the kind of reaction the male will have to this changing role of women and what new experiences we should expect from children and their socialization ties. Youth is viewing, and coming into, a situation that is markedly different from that of its parents. Perhaps we are approaching an age and time where our basic identity and status, our position in society, comes less from our occupational role and more from our recreational role.

This has a number of complications because sex, at least with regard to our parental and grandparental generation, occurred within the recreational framework after most of the energy was expended in an occupational role. We seem to be shifting into a much more recreational era, with much more leisure, and therefore a preoccupation with what to do with this extra time. A lot of the added concern and perhaps dilemma is whether this leisure time is spent with sex or sensual enterprises. Perhaps coming to grips with sex is coming to grips with surplus energy which is not taken up by the occupational role. We will see more and more concern, in a sense, with sexual time and how to deal with it.

The functional and traditional view of man is a situation with sibling position and a specific type of conditioning within the structure itself. A boy without sisters grows up enjoying women but not knowing them in any other sense. In the movie *Carnal Knowledge*, men view women as sex objects when they have no experience with female siblings. The same is true of women raised without male siblings.

Is this a sexual reawakening or perhaps a cyclical thing in society? If it is viewed from a sociological perspective, perhaps it can be said that under certain occurrences in a society we will find more sublimated forms rather than repressed. For example, we see increased aggression in the form of war which is sanctioned. Will we then find increased sexuality which is also liberated? Is what happened in the 60's and 70's a consequence of war, just as what happened in the 20's is a consequence of what happened in World War I? If this is true, perhaps we are reaching a peak and all of these things will gradually die down. This has ramifications; if we view this as something which is going to continue to progress, what if we liberate ourselves and our sexual impulses in therapy? What if, in five years, the whole nature of society has not liberated but has actually regressed, and we live with some of the types of liberation that we expressed at one particular time in our past? Will this come back to haunt us?

The main topic is, whose stake is this? Is this youth's stake or the parents' stake? Or is it the stake of both generations? Is it basically because we are coming into a society which is changing, and youth, because of its input to society, has changed and assimilated some of the things differently than their parents have?

LAUREL

I would like to address myself more directly and specifically to the topic and probably from a little broader basis. One can look at the topic as stated or reverse it and look at it from the stake of the parents in the youth hang-up. Therapy is directed to changing something—toward healing something: This is implicit in what therapy means. Youth is changing, and if a child's sexual behavior appears to be different from his parent's and the situation warrants that the parents and child go to a therapist, what happens? The child sees in his parent's relationship some sort of lack because he is comparing it to something he has read or heard. The reason for a parent saying "side with me" is to preserve what he has chosen to be his values. He wants affirmation of his values because he has chosen to live his life in a certain way. You can see the parents' role another way as saying, "I really want my children to be like me because I really thought about the same things he is doing or thinking and I changed my mind and decided to go back to this because it is a better way. It is more stable. Society will continue to thrive if he chooses my way." Most parental reasons are somewhat negative, even dubious, and the therapist should consider that the child's side has at least optomistic possibilities. The therapist should side with the child but attempt to promote understanding within the family. There is a statement in Gibran about helping the parents teach their children or letting the children be arrows from their bows.

MIKE

I cannot separate what I think from what I live and go through. I would like to talk about some of the things I think I feel. Look at the topic "Youth's Stake in the Sexual Hangups of their Parents"—that says something. Parents' sexual hangups seem to connote something negative. We need to remedy it. It reminds me of a machine with a gear missing, but if we put back the gear, the machine will continue to function and be all right. I cannot look at a person as separate parts. I have to look at a person as something total, as *someone.* Part of the problem we have is with the deep, underlying assumptions about the way people operate. I think it is important that therapists sometimes try to bring in the parents in a therapy session so the children can know how the parents feel.

I also look at a human being as a person with potential for human development and growth. There is always this possibility, and the role I see of a therapist, as Mrs. Satir has said, is helping people to cope. But I do not see only therapists doing that; I think that in interrelationships with each other we help each other to cope and to grow. To me one of the most important ways we learn is when we learn someone else is really interested in us. I look at the fact that my parents have certain problems; these have effected me, and I am going to have certain problems no matter what I do, and they are going to affect my children; however, maybe I can build on the basis my children have given me. Maybe they have inhibited my freedom, but they have given me the opportunity to develop beyond that. I grew up in a very rigid Italian Catholic background. You were told certain things. There was one view of the world and that was it. However, it was not pounded into me too much. I was not beaten over the head with it. I went to parochial school for twelve years. Six or eight years ago, when I started high school, a lot of young people were questioning things, so I got a lot of different perspectives, and this had a big influence on the way I reacted. It started me thinking. I could use some of the basis I had for thinking and relate to my parents, so I could say, okay, my parents had limited sexual relationships. To them it was something that was bad, and they raised children with that idea. They had a child, and that was about all. That was one problem. I cannot separate the sexual hangups of my parents from all the other hangups. They did not relate to each other very well. They still do not. But I do not hate my parents because of that. They did not box me in, and maybe they could have, although maybe in some situations they did. How can I understand my parents and relate to them? I do not have a place in their home anymore. I am an alien in the house back in Brooklyn, but I am glad about that because it makes me love my parents as individuals, as human beings, not as someone who depends on them, but someone who has grown from them, hopefully who can go beyond them. I cannot wipe their rear ends for the rest of my life. I can just try to take what they have given me and do something with it. I would not want to be married as my parents are . . . if it has to be that way, I will not be married. If I do have children, I hope someday I will not understand some of the things my children say. I hope someday my children scare me! Otherwise, I am going nowhere. I hope somehow we can get back to the human element that we can relate to each other. The sexual aspect is important, but it is more than that, and maybe that is where the value change is going.

EILEEN

Fortunately or unfortunately, my approach is a little more sociological than therapeutic even though at one time I was in social work. I looked at the title of the session and thought it was not something that was here and now but a future-oriented thing, because if indeed sexual practices and social aspects of life are changing, then the hang-ups and sexual practices of parents will be changing too. With the youth generation becoming parents in time, they as parents will be dealing with a different structure—a different kind of problem. I have a question as to whether the sexual values are really changing or whether *we* are. I like to consider myself part of the youth generation, and we were socialized in a general pattern which our parents came to first in terms of sexual practices or sexual values. Now as we grow up, we grow up in a different world from what they grew up in in terms of sex, and I question whether our values have changed as they have not been put to a test. We have not socialized another generation yet, and I wonder if when it comes our turn—when we become parents and raise new people for the world—whether we will end up going back to the way we were socialized. It seems to me our parents went back with minor changes to a static situation, to how they were socialized, which is how they maintained a specific social structure. If there has been a change in sexual values, then it seems to me other patterns will change also. The institution of marriage will probably have to change if changing sexual values have occurred; according to the new "youth generation" (that is a Time Magazine idea maybe more than a reality), if they accept the institution of marriage, then they really have not changed any sexual values. It goes beyond sexual values in marriage. It goes into entire world values—world views—which are tied up in this. Are we not assuming something that is not there and would time not be the test of it?

DIANE

I hope you are all doing your part to reduce human suffering— that's "right on." My position is in terms of my own changing social values, how to start changing my life so there will be some sort of future for human beings. As far as our topic is concerned, I do not know whether I really can view it at all. My parents never really talked about whether they were sexually adjusted. I do not even know if they were. Maybe the topic should be turned around and maybe we should discuss why parents have a stake in what they call the sexual adjustments of their children. Maybe, in fact what parents are trying to do—why parents get anxious about their loose sons or daughters—is that their values are coming in question, and this is a scary thing for them; it means the world is changing, and this sticks us all where we are. So I would say that I am more concerned for the future and how I am going to go about coping with that. You have a view of the here and now. People come to you with problems, and you cannot say: "Well, here is a desired future state." You have to work within the specifics of the family, and you have to deal with the family.

In my life, I do not want to deal with the nuclear family as I now see it, so I am trying to work out a life style on my own and with the other people I am living with, that will allow for human potential and development. It was not always that children were seen as different people. In the Middle Ages, they were seen as miniature adults. They were integrated into society at a very early age, as soon as they could start operating. If you read diaries of royal children—the Dauphin of France talked of sexual activity at the age of six. There was not segregation in terms of age the way the social order—the educational order— is now organized. This segregation between age groups makes one lose sight of where one once was: When you are a sixth-grader, you can forget what it is like to be a third-grader. When you are an adult, you have really lost sight of what it is to be a child. What I would like to accomplish just in my own life is for my children to have a sense of themselves at an early age. There is no reason to protect them. They are not all that innocent. They cope with the real world very soon. Parents seem to have a vested interest in keeping this age of innocence because things are so bad now it is nice to look back when things were really fabulous. (But if you remember, things were not really that fabulous!)

JACK

First, I would like to give credit to Dr. Pollak for a lot of my difficulty in coping with problems: Dr. Pollak introduced me to the paradoxes of living. I used to think things were very obvious—where I was and where everyone else was. We were all in nice little boxes and nice status roles. I thank Dr. Pollak for introducing the paradoxes of life!

I have a friend who was a psychiatrist and now makes jewelry and works in leather. He used to do child psychiatry. He found out that he was not doing child psychiatry, he was doing mother psychiatry or parent psychiatry. He would get the child in a therapy situation, and the child would leave him and the mother would come back frantically week after week saying, "How can you say these things about me and are you implying I am sick and have sexual hangups?" He would say, "Yes," and they would go find another therapist. In America we bargain until we find someone who finds out we are sick or our child is sick in the way we want them to be. I come from one area that is a therapist's dream—Miami Beach, Florida. Those therapists who have been to Miami Beach know there is a certain amount of work you can get there, a lot of which has to do with the child. As for the children's stake in their parent's sexual hangups, it is exactly that. A child is put in a therapy situation, and it really becomes a war between his parents' sexual ideas and his ideas of what is proper sexuality and the child's new values as the topic indicates.

The question I would ask, going back to Laurel's particular point of view is: Whose side is the therapist going to be on? Is the therapist going to take sides? One thing I noticed in particular was that therapists, both men and women, are threatened. They are taking sides on the *status quo*. They are saying, that is not what is healthy or that is not the way it ought to be. If you are going to make these moral decisions, I think it is important that we take a much more humanistic point of view: We start observing ourselves and see what the child or young person has to say about his sexuality, attempting to see it through his eyes. As I listen to some of the things people are saying, I think some of your basic assumptions are based on formulae: "What Freud said," or we have a convenient label, "ways of copping out." I was also very gratified that Virginia Satir proceeded to tell me at least what therapists are about because I was not terribly sure. I was beginning to get the idea that therapy meant conformity when it becomes parent versus child, especially regarding sexuality. The way to get the child out of the problem is to make him conform and that conformity is indeed help. Actually, I am still not sure that that is not what help really is—that conformity really becomes help. You certainly do not have people with anxiety who are total conformers, not in its most ideal sense. The children are indeed changing in terms of sexual values, if they are evaluating their own parents' sexuality as incomplete or if they find love and peace generated. This is quite old. Christ was a love-and-peace man. The young people are clear that the institutions we support and the church systems do not epitomize Christ. For myself, I think I see through it. I prefer to deal with people on a one-to-one basis, attempting to encounter them and attempting to feel them out. I think this is the therapist's duty as well. I do not think you can put people in boxes; I do not think you can put them into formulae. I think you have to deal with them, and especially the child, as you relate to them. You cannot make judgments that he is sick or well until you are able to understand and put yourself in his position in terms of his own sexual mores. Another reason I am so adamant about this is that everybody knows psychiatric terms. I walk into a classroom and people start telling me they are neurotic. It reminds me of the self-fulfilling prophecy. Are you alienated until someone tells you what alienated means? Then all of a sudden you walk around saying, "My God, I'm alienated." The first-year medical student finds out he has every disease because he has every symptom. So I would remind you—I see the therapists, the psychiatrist, psychologist, family therapist, as indeed becoming the new priests. And in this context, people are going to be turning to them to find out what is right or—it is not going to be good or bad anymore—what is sick, sick and healthy. I would also like to reiterate what Diane was saying about day care and pre-school children, that the child will not be around the parents very much. Thus he will not be able to see his parents' sexual hangups, and the idea of peer influence might be much more important in the future.

WHAT DO I DO AS A THERAPIST?

Commentary: Virginia Satir

In thinking about what I do as a therapist, the best answer I can come up with is: "I use myself in the best way I know to make it possible for you, whoever you are, to grow." I have been struck over and over by the fact that in Situation A, a man has something going with a woman other than his wife, yet the same thing going on in Situations X, Y, and Z can have completely different consequences! As long as I have been around, there is nothing that says the situation is the same as the *meaning* of the situation. I have thought of myself as someone who assists in bringing about new copings, so in the lives of many people as presented to me, there was this affair or that one. My question is not *why* the affair as such, but at this moment in time, "What is the meaning to you as you tell it to me now, and what are you telling me about yourself at this moment that bothers you?" I work almost entirely with the idea that we are constantly reshaping our feelings of worth, and if there is something awesome, in my opinion, it has to do with self-worth and with really coming in touch with ourselves as creatures who can be decision-makers. Now what does that really consist of? Sometimes I hear that we do not have to deal with some of the issues of our self-worth if we have a structure around us, but some of the old structures are not predictable anymore. In thinking about myself, I cannot be separated either from values, but I think I like being able to be separated from telling others that they should be like me. Years ago as a therapist, I was cautioned: "You should not follow up people's lives with your life." I learned after awhile that I was actually doing a disservice by the way I was withholding, that is, because I said something that fitted for me in the way I looked at things,

169

that could be part of a whole resource for a new potential model. But that is not where the problem is; the problem is the attitude expressed in: "The right way to do it is the way I tell you." In a funny kind of way, I have a hunch that one thing bugging us here is that part of the therapeutic philosophy which we all know is that we are rebringing up people to have new images of themselves, but we ought to have some kind of plan about the old parental business. Perhaps it is not that overt, but I think it is probably true.

When I look back at myself over the last thirty years and at different periods of my life, I might have told you that my values are now different as far as structure is concerned. But there is one value that has been growing all along the way; it has two main parts. One has to do with my feeling of worth about myself as a productive, attractive human being. The second part has to do with the fact of my aloneness. Those two things add up to something which I find is behind me. Many of the problems that people have in meeting different kinds of situations are related to the fact that there is a kind of filter we look through to see all that people do. I am quite aware at this point—and have been more aware ever since I left the completely clinical situation I used to have—that thousands of people are doing things, and coming off okay—things which in my clinical practice do not come off okay. So it is not the situation but the unique experiences around us. I think this is an important point to remember. Many of us know that in a funny way, our reference point, particularly in the group psychotherapy and medical model, is looking at life through the eyes of the sick, and what we have as alternatives to that are little pieces of experience in our own life which do not really add up to another kind of reference point. I suppose the thrilling excitement to me at this point in time is finding many people who look at the same pieces of behavior quite differently! I want to look more fully myself when I am practicing therapy as a therapist at what I call a *change-character*. I want to look with completely open eyes at the coping aspects of the person, not with what he is doing. For this means a person is in touch with his own ability to cope and can use his own resources, knowing he has choices, and that person is probably going to be a pretty productive, creative, and attractive person.

DR. ISRAEL CHARNEY

I want to express my appreciation for the sense of balance and structure that I hear in this panel. A number of people have addressed themselves to the paradoxes of change, the sobriety of change, the possibility of more Messiahs, indeed the hope, the possibility that the children of the next generation and many generations will answer many questions. I would like to give some supporting data from a recent visit to a kibbutz a few weeks ago. This had reference to communal life and the change process, both economic possibilities and the opportunity for change that marks all generational developments, raising the question of whether to continue the children's house or whether the children would be living with their parents as they had not heretofore. The controversy was a momentous one. The kibbutz was literally split open. Many observers noted that as the discussion began there was a distinct generation gap between the generation who had grown up in the children's house and the parents of the previous generation who had had their children grow up in the children's house. The gap was as follows: The children who had grown up in the children's house are now voting overwhelmingly that their children be permitted to live with them. They remembered with great bitterness in this very lovely kibbutz all sorts of aspects of their own experience. What this example argues for is that every generation is necessarily going to argue with those patterns of child-rearing that they have experienced. There is no pattern known to man that can eliminate certain fundamentals in the human process—anxiety and confrontation with one's aloneness, the absurdities of life, the paradoxes of life. This leads to a number of implications for group life, sexual life, and family life.

CARLTON ORCHINIK

I do not think any of these speakers so far has shown that they are content. They may well be happy but they are not content! Here are some wind-up comments from our guest speaker.

VIRGINIA SATIR

When I was five, I wanted to be a children's detective on parents. This is where it all started. I was aware. I was the oldest child of five (I have a pair of twin brothers eighteen months younger than myself). I am not prepared to say all that went into that desire, but I am prepared to say that I remember as though it were yesterday that that is where I wanted my life to go. It meant to enter the puzzle of things I could not make sense of, things that were out of my reach. And also, things that had to do with things I did not even know about except that I knew there were things I did not even know about! I lived quite a long time before I became aware that I was really pretty profound at age five. I went through some parts of my life where I thought I knew. That is where I died a little.

As we come to the close of this meeting, a few things strike me. I have whole new areas to think about. It pleases me because I am excited. When I am looking to go somewhere, it does not mean without pain, and as has been said, we do not live life without pain. We never really "have it made," as such. It seems to me that the two things that happen in therapy are kinds of pleas . . . "Can I really hear you—Can you really hear me?" I can remember that happening in families I have worked with when it is crystal clear that each person is making a bridge to another person in terms of his personhood. It can be any two human beings connecting, whether it is a four-year-old with a ninety-year-old or a ten- and a twelve-year-old, and at that point there is no more in the way of hypocrisy. We all come to that point of knowing that from the time we are born to the time we die, we feel helpless at times and angry at times and then to the knowledge that one of us has a whole different role because of one's humanness. The other point has to do with the fact that as human beings, we may be evolving to a point just reserved for saints now that there is more to the human being than we have allowed ourselves to see in the past, that searching for fulfillment is part of what we are looking for here. I want to express my joy for first being asked to come here and for the experiences I have had with you all. I feel you have enriched my life.

CARLTON ORCHINIK

We have now come to the end of another discussion which has run the full gamut of experiences in many ways. We have suffered part of the time, we have felt threatened, we have fallen asleep, we have lived a little. We have fought with each other sometimes. Perhaps the same thoughts have been expressed many times. But maybe we are a little closer now. It is difficult for an audience this size to feel this. I know the Family Institute members look for this. They do not expect to agree with each other. This makes for a good working, loving group. We are part of a family too. Despite our differences, fights, incongruencies we work and stay together and love each other. I hope the rest of you will feel the same way.

INDEX

A

Abortion, 11, 39
Ackerman, Nathan, 80
  First Memorial Address (1971), 8-18
  Third Annual Memorial Address (1973), 144-157
Affairs, extramarital, 54, 60, 135
  and therapist's values, 129
  consequences of, 64
  reactions to, 62
  secrecy concerning, 65
Alexander, Franz, 29
"Alligator maneuver," 4
Aloneness, 170
Anxieties, sexual, 66, 114
Arcologies, defined, 50
Arcosanti, 47, 47
Assertiveness, within marriage, 119
Attitudes, sexual,
  changing nature of, 9, 13, 17

B

Bach, George, 68
"Balance of power," male-female, 119
Behavioral control, 19
Beneficiary, re-evaluation of position of, 38
Betz, Barbara, 149
Bigamous marriage, 76
Birth control, 39
  pill, 10
Blue laws, 39
Bowen, Murray, 65, 88

C

Castration, fear of, 125
Change-character, 170

Change, paradoxes of, 171
  social impact of, 28
Childbirth process, 11
Children, alternative modes of rearing, 101
  as source of compensatory happiness, 160
  in process of separation and divorce, 78
City living, 50
Class prejudice, 31
Commitment, in marriage, 72
Communal marriage, 12, 76
Communication, faulty,
  as source of sexual dysfunction, 117
  indirect, in family therapy, 137
  lack of, 68
  openness within family, 20
Community Mental Health Centers, 49
Community structure,
  relation to family therapy, 46
Compromise, capacity for, 76
Continuity, of experience, 35
Cooper, David, 133
Corporate marriage, 76
Co-therapists, in couples group therapy, 69
Counseling, 24
Counter-therapy, 24
Counter-transference, in marital therapy, 60
Couple therapy, 54, 120
Couple-unit, and inadequate ego, 116
Couples group therapy, 54, 68

D

Denial, in marital therapy, 61
Density of suburban living, 45
Dependency needs, within marriage, 77

175